AF653842

Changing Demands of

Technical and Vocational Education

Changing Demands of Technical and Vocational Education

Indira Madhukar

AUTHORSPRESS

Worldwide Circulation through Authorspress Global Network
First Published 2003
by Authorspress

E-35/103, Jawahar Park
Laxmi Nagar, Delhi-110 092

e-mail: authorspress@yahoo.com

Copyright © 2003 Authorspress

Typeset in NewCenturySchlbk by Chitra Computers

Changing Demands of Technical and Vocational Education
ISBN 81-7273-142-6

Printed in India at Tarun Offset, Delhi.

Preface

Globalisation and the revolution in information and communication technology have signalled the need for a new human-centred development paradigm. The Technical and Vocational Education (TVE), as an integral component of lifelong learning, has a crucial role to play in this new era as an effective tool to realise the objectives of a culture of peace, environmentally sound, sustainable development, social cohesion, and international citizenship.

TVE is most directly concerned with the acquisition of the knowledge and skills required for the world of work, formal and informal, urban and rural. One of the most notable characteristics of the changing face of vocational-technical education will be the elimination of the traditional tracking systems. No longer will students be identified and/or categorised as academic college bound, traditional or vocational. The educational delivery system will provide a continuum of academic and vocational opportunities for all students so they are prepared to meet the demands of employment and lifelong learning.

Every country must adapt its TVE programme to cater to the skill requirements of its workplace of the twenty-first century. Mindful of the opportunities that lie ahead of us and those which will progressively unfold, and cognizant of the policies, partnerships and resources needed to raise the status and broaden the traditional vision of Technical and Vocational Education, we need to recognise the need for strengthened international partnerships, and particularly to address the needs of developing countries. There is a need to introduce the required changes in a manner suitable for each country, so as to empower and engage human beings in the context of the new paradigm, with TVE as a common key focus of the reform process.

The prerequisites of the TVE response to the new paradigm include appropriate societal values and attitudes, embracing the new technologies, making new policy and financial commitments, and taking account local, regional, and global opportunities and concerns. The relevance and quality of vocational education and training will undoubtedly be enhanced by learning from each other across national borders.

This book discusses the changing demands of the labour market and the consequent changes in the TVE system. It argues that the existing policies of the TVE system should be reshaped to accommodate the new demands of the networked globalised world. It examines different education and training modes, and explores the relationship between kinds of skilled training programmes and social and economic development priorities.

For all career and technical educators, students and policy makers this publication will be a helpful resource. It guides instructors through a curriculum revision process that is based on identifying skill proficiencies that address demands of the changing labour markets. It aims to provide general information to interested parties from abroad.

Editor

Contents

1
Concepts and Tendencies of Vocational Education

Vocational education is of increasing concern to governments as well as in many countries, to industry. This renewed interest is often due to adverse economic and financial conditions, but it is also linked to the search for cost-effectiveness in a context of intense international competition. Over the past decade many countries have been forced to introduce economic adjustment and stabilisation policies. Such programmes have had serious effects on patterns by which governments financc education.

In many cases, adjustments led to drastic measures aimed at minimising government spending and transferring costs to other actors. It is difficult to measure the bulk of spending allocated to vocational education and training. Official data, such as those published by UNESCO, usually refer to central government expenditures, overlooking spending made by decentralised units, such as local governments which, in certain countries, may play a significant role in financing training.

In addition, the integrated nature of secondary education in some systems does not allow for the easy differentiation between the vocational and general components. In fact, the lack of clear definitions makes it difficult to produce comparative data. Finally, a large share of investment in vocational education, by companies and individuals, often remains invisible. As data on the different sources of financing are not always recorded in an exact manner, it is possible that the overall financial effort involved in training is underestimated.

In a context of financial scarcity, vocational education has to provide clear evidence of economic and social returns. In many countries, such evidence is lacking, which is threatening the sustainability of the system and leading to a thorough questioning of vocational education. Vocational education has been an important component of international assistance to education. However, project support has often been preferred to a more integrated sectoral approach. Recent shifts in international assistance seem to seek sustainability through a long- term strategic approach.

Current directions include institutional capacity-building, strengthening private training and training by the employer, improving the management and efficiency of public institutions as well as their capacity to raise funds. Although the reference to so-called 'models' is frequent, the overall management and coordination of national training systems is quite varied, ranging from centralised planning to market-oriented regulation. Similarly, financing training modes are very diverse and far more complicated than a simple choice between public spending and earmarked payroll taxes.

Such a diversity, combined with the constant evolution of national systems, makes overall comparisons somehow difficult. However, it is worthwhile identifying and analysing the range of options available. Wide recognition that the state can no longer assume alone the financial burden of vocational education has led to the development of new modes of government intervention such as cost-sharing and subsidiarity.

The effort of governments to share the cost of education, including vocational education, with other members of society has now become a global phenomenon, affecting both developing countries and industrialised nations. Apart from being an expression of cold pragmatism—compensating for the decrease in government spending—cost sharing corresponds to the belief that the financial burden of education should be distributed among all beneficiaries. Hence, employers and individuals who take advantage of higher productivity and income should contribute to the cost of vocational education. Implementation of the cost-sharing principle has led to the introduction of a diversity of measures, such as student fees, employer sponsorship of trainees, technology-transfer grants and contracts from industry, sale of continuing education services, sale of other products and services.

Deferred payment through the use of loans has also been considered as a promising way of securing resources from students, based upon their future income. In the field of vocational education it seeks to uphold the local dimension of the training system or, at least, the relevance of training provision *vis-a-vis* the needs of local labour markets. Therefore, within a decentralised framework, financing training should be organised according to the principle of subsidiarity, the central state only supporting programmes that cannot be efficiently covered by lower entities, for instance, those considered to be critical for industrial development strategies or those aimed at vulnerable groups.

However, in practice, even assuming that local governments have a comparative advantage in providing training, the huge differences observed in tax base at this level would hardly ensure an adequate amount of finance. Hence, the central government may retain the role of harmonising funding in order to guarantee minimum standards across the country. In spite of the far-reaching implications of cost-sharing and subsidiarity, many economic justifications remain for the subsidising of vocational education services. First, benefits are not only captured by individuals or firms, but have a spillover effect on the entire society. Indeed, assuming that most initial training is transferable, vocational education may be considered as a quasi-collective good, just like general education. Secondly, economies of scale can only be achieved through providing services to a significant share of the population.

Finally, in the absence of sufficient knowledge of the costs and benefits of alternative forms of education, it is doubtful whether individuals or enterprises are able to make the best decisions. This lack of information would then lead, at the macro level, to a state of under-investment in training. In addition to the economic rationale, it is arguable that leaving the vocational education of the disadvantaged groups in society entirely to what they could buy on the open market would be socially unacceptable.

Private institutions tend to make an increasing contribution to training. They constitute a very heterogeneous sector, difficult to define and to clearly delineate. Legal status, ownership, objectives, operations and, of course, financing are some of the criteria differentiating private vocational schools and training centres. Tuition fees, paid by individuals or enterprises, usually represent a significant, if not a major source of income. However, in many countries, private institutions also benefit from government financial allocations and tax incentives. Institutions linked to NGOs may raise a significant share of their resources through donations. It is arguable that private training institutions constitute a market-financed response to a growing social demand.

Apart from reducing reliance on the state budget, it is hoped that the private sector can promote fair competition, eventually leading to cost reduction. Yet, the quality of training given by this sector varies immensely from one institution to the other. In fact, the variation in quality may be much wider within the private sector than for public institutions that have to meet certain standards. It is doubtful that this issue of quality control can be resolved by pure market mechanisms.

In many countries, governments are developing information on training supply and trying to regulate the training market by introducing accreditation and monitoring mechanisms for private institutions. Apart from the quality issue, private provision raises the question of access for low- income groups. A fair system should make provision to grant financial assistance to students from the poorest families. Furthermore, past experience has shown that private institutions have a tendency to invest in 'cheap to teach' subjects, leaving programmes requiring heavy infrastructures to government.

The market approach to vocational education does not only lead to the development of private institutions, it also has an impact on the way public institutions are managed and financed. In particular, it is argued that market incentives provide a better manner of allocating resources. Apart from the introduction of cost-recovery measures, this policy advocates giving institutions autonomy over programmes, admissions and financial resources.

Increasing financial autonomy may also encourage public institutions to develop income-generating activities and seek local solidarity through strengthening links with businesses and communities in their environment. Besides attracting donations in cash or kind, such a strategy is meant to improve the capacity of institutions to assess training needs at the local level. Increasing accountability is usually the counterpart of more autonomy. In the context of a decentralised and competitive framework, institution managers are encouraged to move away progressively from the traditional pattern of basing budget estimates on allocations of previous years, in favour of a system based on performance.

Introducing the use of vouchers can offer an alternative way of allocating funds to training institutions. In line with the principle of consumer-paid services, this mode of intervention reflects a major shift towards a demand-driven formula. This funding arrangement, based on output rather than on input, requires, among other things, that individuals and enterprises be fully informed of the programmes of institutions and their performance.

However, their large-scale use would introduce instability and eventually threaten the sustainability of the training system. Whatever the mechanism might be, the allocation of public money to institutions enjoying greater autonomy inevitably raises the issue of control. The market-feedback system is often said to be the most effective. Nevertheless, some reservations can be made concerning its reliability, taking into consideration the information problem and the need to follow certain national objectives, such as the promotion of labour mobility or giving priority to specific groups.

International data tend to show that, although general taxation still represents, in most instances, a major source of funding, especially for initial training, earmarked taxation now constitutes a significant option. It usually takes the form of a payroll tax and finds its justification in the equity principle, which stipulates that enterprises should be responsible for the cost of the education which is of direct benefit to them. Although the human capital theory indicates that enterprises benefit from investment in training, they may actually underinvest due to the so-called 'poaching effect'.

According to the country, available data indicate that the rate of the levy varies from 0.5 per cent to 4 per cent of the payroll. In some cases, it also changes according to sectors of the economy and size of the enterprise's workforce. The public sector as well as small enterprises are often exempted. The introduction, and sometimes abandonment, of a financing scheme based on payroll tax depends very much on specific considerations, such as the availability of skills and training, the overall structure and weight of the tax system, the cost of labour, and the strength of the consensus between the state, employers and the wider community regarding the necessity and use of a training levy.

The main criticism of payroll taxes lies in their inflationary effect on labour costs. This concern is particularly strong when fiscal and social levies on labour are already high. Eventually, using payroll as the basis for the training tax might have other macro-economic effects. In particular, such a system produces a distortion between labour-intensive and capital-intensive enterprises that could supposedly affect investment patterns and, in the long run, the economic structure.

The introduction of payroll tax has led to the creation and wide dissemination of a new type of institution often managed by both the public and private sectors, sometimes also involving unions through a tripartite formula. These bodies or Training Funds, which collect and allocate the resources raised by the tax, combine financial and training responsibilities. In some cases, financing and promoting training are the major objectives of such institutions. In others, the Fund is incorporated into a broader Training Agency or Board which also operates its own training system, parallel to the vocational streams of the education sector, and sometimes decides upon the national training policy. Indeed, giving the management of Training Funds to the social partners can contribute to the enhancement of the quality, relevance and flexibility of training.

The central Fund model is not the only option, and some countries have established sectoral bodies. Mostly applied in the developing world, the use of a large centralised Fund tends to redistribute training costs between training and non-training firms. Sectoral Funds can better meet the requirements of well organised sectors of the economy or facilitate dealing with specific manpower or qualification shortages.

The collectivisation, or mutualisation, of resources allowed by the Funds, especially central Funds, helps in the development of a collectively agreed training strategy aimed at specific types of firms, sectors, categories of workers or regions. This option can be a very powerful instrument for promoting both equity and effectiveness. In financial terms, this redistributive function is made possible by introducing a formula, whereby individual firms have access to only one portion of their contribution to finance their own training.

The balance remains accumulated in a collective account put at the disposal of the Fund to finance programmes decided upon by its governing body. It is important to note that, for many institutions, accumulated savings constitute a stabilisation fund that can be used to finance capital investment or face a drop in payroll tax collection. Usually, nationwide

Funds both levy for their own training policy and make grants to training firms. Progressively, many of them have developed their activities to provide, on a cost-recovery basis, consultancy services to enterprises in the field of human resources development. They also often play a key role in regulating the training market by introducing accreditation procedures and quality control for private training institutions.

It is widely felt that investing in technical and vocational education and training contributes to economic growth, as reflected in the above country examples. In particular, this form of human capital formation supposedly facilitates technological change and international competitiveness. At the same time, and in spite of the absence of clear statistical evidence, there is a feeling that societies underinvest in training. This attitude is suspected to be widespread in industry, where individual enterprises often tend to prefer poaching skilled workers. Such so-called "market failures" require public intervention, although there is strong international support in favour of the allocation of resources through market forces.

The issue then becomes to determine how governments can best design financing policies in order to improve the efficiency and effectiveness of technical education and training. Specific aspects concern the possibility of defining appropriate cost-sharing arrangements and ways of conceiving effective incentive structures. In spite of their wide economic, social and cultural differences, the countries selected here illustrate some of the major trends affecting the financing of technical and vocational education and training systems worldwide.

Financial diversification is observed in most countries, reflecting either an effort to shift financing towards a more market-driven pattern or to change workers' and employers' attitude, as reflected in the case studies. This strategy also frequently corresponds to a forced adjustment to shrinking public budgets. The introduction of fees and the use of general or earmarked taxation represent various possible market, state or collaborative instruments to diversify resources.

The examples show that there is no pure model, and that financing systems fluctuate from state to market regulation over a period of time within a specific country. The need and/ or the wish to diversify finances forms one of the main reasons for such fluctuations. Foreign aid, through grants and loans, also constitutes, in many countries, like in the Côte d'Ivoire and Mauritius, a significant element in the initial support of the gradual restructuring of national financing systems..

The performance of Korea and Singapore in regulating labour markets cannot be attributed to efficient market mechanisms. In trying to understand these successes, increasing interest is being paid to the role played by specific social institutions. Among these, Training Funds and Boards deserve special attention, especially when assuming that skill development is a precondition for sustained growth. In most selected examples, the financing system relies on a Fund, sometimes incorporated within a broader Board, which plays a central role in the allocation of resources, partly raised by a payroll tax. This institutional arrangement is currently in place, or being considered, in many developing countries.

It is possible to identify three functions performed by Training Funds: banking, mutual funding and insurance. As in a bank, enterprises can withdraw from their account funds required to cover their training expenditures: this constitutes the basic function of Training Funds.

The redistributive function, present in many systems, made possible by the constitution of mutual funds, contributes towards tackling the needs of disadvantaged workers, enterprises or regions. Finally, enterprises facing sudden technological change may be able to benefit from the Funds' accumulated savings to finance emergency training programmes. To this extent, the payroll tax can represent a form of mandatory savings account, which can offer additional protection to enterprises requiring greater training-related financial support at certain stages of their development.

Getting together all the institutions involved in the decisions that affect them is increasingly considered an efficient approach towards improving the functioning of training systems. Participation of stakeholders means giving them the institutional capacity to influence policy making and management as well as to control activities and resources. Reforming the financing mechanisms must be seen against the broader context of redefining the responsibilities of the main economic agents *vis-a-vis* technical and vocational education and training systems.

Over and above the financial participation of employers by way of the payroll tax and fiscal incentives, public policies also reflect an effort to modify the role of the state in training and to achieve a new social contract between the different partners involved. In this respect, Training Funds or Boards represent an important locus in forging an agreement between the state, employers and individuals regarding policy issues as well as their respective role in training.

Complementary trends concern the participation of local governments and NGOs, especially in the context of decentralisation and territorial development policies. Finally, the challenge of partnership is to ensure that the main actors involved in the productive sector are committed to the principle of investing in human capital formation, and acknowledge its importance for development. However, partnership does present some costs and risks. Participation and dialogue involve time. In practice, partnership often slows down the decision-making process.

A kind of trade-off occurs between the adoption of a participatory approach and being able to make fast decisions. Short-term management objectives may favour the handiness of the system, while a sustainable training strategy would require the sharing of control. Increasing the number of actors involved is also subject to cultural and political limitations. In some cases, labour representatives may be perceived as threats. Therefore, although often praised, increased partnership still encounters much resistance.

The level of economic development constitutes a major constraint for the financing system. In particular, the extent to which the state can share the cost of training with other partners is directly linked to the structure of the economy. If the possibilities of introducing and operating a payroll tax-funded system are high in middle-income and high-income countries, it may be more problematic in a low-income economy.

Below a certain scale the benefits of the levy-based system are necessarily limited due to the impossibility of initiating an accumulation process. In this respect, it must be underlined that the pay-roll-tax system is tailored to address the needs of a modern economy. Its capacity to consolidate skills in the informal sector is minimal. The role of the State in the economy has an influence on financing policies. Financial diversification corresponds to an era dominated by a global shift to a market economy.

In many countries, such a predominant strategy also forms part of a broader response to an unprecedented fiscal crisis. However, under certain circumstances, financing strategies for training may contradict economic policies. It is notably the case in the use of payroll taxes in a context of fiscal austerity. Indeed, taxation becomes a sensitive issue in a process of economic liberalisation, when resource allocation is increasingly meant to be driven by market signals. Facing the pressure for more fiscal orthodoxy, the use of payroll tax, as compared to general taxation, can appear questionable.

The performance of a given financing system will very much depend on the attitude of individuals and employers regarding training. The introduction of a payroll levy may be viewed by employers as just another tax. Making them aware of the associated incentives and of the potential impact of training on labour productivity may call for intensive and long periods of consultation. Incentive structures for investing in training are based upon the assumption that the willingness and strategy of firms and individuals depend largely on the cost factor.

When making investment decisions in training, enterprises may take into account a number of elements, including the business cycle, technological change and also industrial relations. Nevertheless, reforming the financing system certainly constitutes a way of changing the attitude of the various actors.

Highly conflicting situations are hardly conducive to positive dialogue. They are more likely to lead to hostile confrontation. It is obviously difficult to manage a training system under such conditions. A pragmatic approach to this problem might mean the exclusion of certain parties from the governing body of the Funds. It could also be argued that the full participation of the social partners in labour institutions, including Training Funds, can contribute to the collective organisation of the various parties and later facilitate training-policy dialogue with government.

In order to be effective, financial diversification policies must benefit from a strong institutional framework. This is especially the case for payroll tax that requires a reliable administrative machinery to ensure that tax recovery is effective.

Payroll taxes are usually collected by the Income Tax Department of the Ministry of Finance, together with other company taxes, or by the national insurance scheme, which already raises social contributions. In both cases, a sound institutional capacity to collect an additional tax is required. The performance of a Training Fund depends in part on its administrative cost. The selected experiences indicate that the operation of a tax rebate or reimbursement schemes requires extensive processing for grant or exemption applications. Often, malfunctioning bureaucracy leads to delayed payment and to a loss of confidence in the system.

Depending on the magnitude of economies of scale, the average cost would be relatively lower for large systems, given the number of contributing enterprises. In small, low-income countries, lacking strong taxing and regulatory capabilities, a simple financing system would minimise collection, record-keeping, pay-out and other administrative costs. Although it would be harmful to establish a link between legal status and administrative efficiency, experience has shown that, in certain environments, publicly managed Funds run a higher risk of encouraging wasteful spending.

The objective can be either to raise funds for training or to change attitudes. In some cases, objectives go beyond the training issue to affect further dimensions, such as the choice of technology. A distinction can be made between the systems based upon compulsory requirements and those using incentive instruments. Incentive structures are based on a tax rebate or a training grant. Compulsory instruments usually take the form of a payroll tax; less frequent is the enforcement of a quota for training.

Government resources are usually used to finance a public system for technical education or vocational initial and continuing training. They are also used to support programmes designed for disadvantaged groups. Over and above these specific objectives, training systems and their financing can be considered within a macro-economic and educational perspective. For instance, financing training can be part of a public policy aimed at reducing investors' risks. In another context, heavy investments in training can be viewed as an effort to compensate for the low quality of basic education.

Training Funds, especially when they enjoy substantial financial surpluses, constitute a hidden and exclusive source of income. As such, they represent a tempting prey for a government budget under pressure, especially when they are publicly managed. As the concept of earmarked taxation is alien to orthodox fiscal doctrine and often contradictory to fundamental public finance principles, it is difficult to establish legitimately a complete separation between payroll-generated income and the state budget. In many African countries, this partly explains why the apprenticeship tax is, in fact, never used to finance training but allocated to other, less clearly defined purposes.

Although macro-economic empirical evidence is still lacking for training levies, common sense tells us that high payroll taxes mean fewer jobs. Furthermore, it is argued that the growth of the informal sector labour force is partly due to excessive payroll taxes. Hence, evasion not only undermines the sustainability of the financing system but also affects the structure and competitiveness of the economy, labour productivity being usually lower in the informal sector.

Heavy investments in technical and vocational education and training often correspond to a policy for democratising education and broadening training opportunities. In addition to expanding secondary education by developing vocational tracks, or providing alternative, non-formal forms of education, this policy has also led to compensatory government programmes. These schemes, sometimes supported by industry, are aimed at disadvantaged groups in the labour markets.

Early school dropouts, minorities, and informal sector workers, often form part of these targeted populations. Such training schemes also constitute an important component of poverty-alleviation policies or "active" labour-market progra-mmes. The rationale inspiring these policies seems sound against a background of high structural unemployment: providing the jobless with the skills required by the economy should improve the labour market situation. Similarly, if one accepts that wages are linked to labour productivity, to train people for qualified jobs should contribute to reducing poverty. In reality, the results of these policies are mixed and often disappointing, especially in periods of high unemployment.

In spite of the fact that there is little empirical evidence to support such intervention, such questions remain open. Some argue that, taking into account the high cost of training, social objectives and equity would be better addressed by improving the overall educational level of the population through increased investment in basic and general education. Improving the "trainability" of people through higher quality education would eventually diminish training costs, especially as the science and technology content of general education is on the increase. It seemed fair to consider that enterprises should contribute towards the direct financing of work-related education and training.

This basic demarcation between general education, on one side, and technical and vocational education and training, on the other, has long served, with some variations, as the guiding mark in defining financing responsibilities and mechanisms. While general education increasingly includes technological contents, the requirement of vocational skills tends to become less applicable to specific, narrowly defined, occupations.

The use of similar technologies across a variety of sectors constitutes a major factor explaining this shift away from job-specific abilities. In addition, the progressive transformation of work organisation, relying less on the principles of Taylorism than it used to, increasingly involves workers in process improvement and quality control.

Although this trend may be mainly affecting capital and knowledge-intensive industries, it already has a strong impact on the way skill formation and industrial learning are being addressed and financed. In the long run, the continuation of this tendency, and its dissemination to an increasing number of countries, as a result of intense international competition, may require reconsidering the concept of technical and vocational education and, therefore, reassessing the premises underlying the classical financing paradigm.

REFERENCES

Ananda, S.M., and S. Rabinowitz, *Developing a Comprehensive Occupational Certification System*, 1995.

American Vocational Association, *The American Vocational Association's Recommendations for Investment in and Improvement of Vocational-Technical Education*, 1997.

Border B., and C. Losh, *Occupational Skill Standards: State Development and Use Systems*, 1996.

Caillods, F., "Converging trends amidst diversity vocational training systems", *International Labour Review,* Vol. 133, no. 2, Geneva, ILO, 1994.

Cinterfor, ILO, "Vocational training on the threshold of the 1990s", *PHREE Background Paper Series, Document No. PHREE/91/35*, Washington, D.C.: World Bank, 1991.

Pring, R., "Liberal Education and Vocational Preparation", pp 49-78 in Barrow, &. White, (eds.) *Beyond Liberal Education: Essays in Honour of Paul H. Hirst* (London: Routledge), 1993.

________________ , *Closing the Gap: Liberal Education and Vocational Preparation*, London: Hodder and Stoughton, 1995.

2

Changing Demands of Technical and Vocational Education

Technical and Vocational Education and Training (TVET), or Vocational Education in brief, should be dealt with, and its issues approached, within the more comprehensive concept of Human Resources Development, a concept that comprises the supply side or sources of human power, as well as the linkages and channels between the supply and demand sides of human power. The supply side covers, as is well known, such sources as the various levels and fields of formal and non-formal education and training systems, including vocational education. It also covers additions to the labour force from external sources such as immigrant labour.

The linkages between the supply and demand sides of human power, on the other hand, which should be considered essential elements of the concept of human resources development, comprise such components as information systems, legislative tools, occupational classifications and standards, employment services, career guidance and counselling services, research and development in the concerned fields, and the relevant institutional setups in the form of councils, boards, committees and administrative units. Considering its nature, content and methodology, vocational education is strongly rooted in educational ideals and objectives, on the one hand, and is thoroughly permeated by labour market criteria and work standards, on the other.

To ensure both the human and professional aspects of vocational education, two major dimensions should always guide the design of the relevant schemes and systems: Education and Work. The educational dimension caters more for the individual needs and human aspects, while the work or economic dimension caters more for societal needs and labour market requirements. Furthermore, modern approaches take it for granted that vocational education schemes and programmes cannot be designed to correspond accurately to a particular job.

The dynamics and changing demand of the labour market require more and more the replacement of physical skills by mental skills, and hence that such schemes and programmes be liberalised and broad-based, to promote adaptability, widen the scope of job opportunities, and enhance educational and occupational mobility.

One of the major challenges that is still encountered by policy makers and planners of vocational education systems, in developing as well as developed countries, is the ability to operationalise the concept of integration, rather than just that of coordination and coexistence, of educational and work values and standards, and hence the integration of individual and societal needs, interests and objectives.

The schism or separation between the education system and the world of work, which is found in particular in most developing countries, is one of the major weaknesses of vocational education systems in these countries.

In many countries, especially industrialised ones, the centre of gravity of vocational education systems is generally located nearer to societal and labour market needs, at the expense of educational values and individual needs. In many other countries, especially developing ones, the centre of gravity is located nearer to educational criteria and standards, at the expense of labour market needs and employment requirements.

SOCIAL STATUS OF VOCATIONAL EDUCATION

The social status of vocational education in any society is, to a great extent, a reflection of the status of work values in that society. Traditional cultures and philosophies range between two extremes regarding their assessment of work values. At one extreme, the ancient Greek culture viewed work as a low-grade life activity that, nevertheless, cannot be dispensed with; while at the other extreme, the Marxist culture viewed work as the supreme value. Between these two extremes, different cultures vary to some extent in their assessment of work values.

A rational and balanced approach can be realised if work activities are assessed both by their material and economic returns on the individual and society, on the one hand, and their social and humanising influences, on the other. Thus, vocational education systems and schemes should be designed as developmental life experiences that have their own social dimension and cultural extension.

Vocational education, should do more than provide the learner with the specific skills and knowledge needed for the job. It should be acknowledged that occupations are more effectively performed by workers who are generally, as well as specifically prepared, taking into consideration the ongoing transformation of work processes, technologies and environments. The social status of vocational education can, on the other hand, be enhanced in practice through appropriate career guidance and counselling services, as well as employment and placement services. Unfortunately, these two types of services are weak in most developing countries, accentuating more the status issues of vocational education.

When such services exist, fully or partially, in developing or developed countries, it is not unusual for the providers of such services to fall in the trap of being guided more by labour market needs and employment priorities, than by the fulfilment of the individual's needs and inclinations, and the realisation of his potentialities. Proper career guidance and employment services should fulfil both labour market and individual needs, and should not end up by adjusting or even distorting the learner's inclinations to labour market requirements. In practice, the social status of vocational education is also influenced, to a great extent, by the type of relation and nature of channels that link it with higher education that leads to the preparation of professionals.

Successful vocational education schemes are usually designed with inherent and built-in links with higher educational and occupational levels, through the formal or non-formal systems of education, within the general concept of continuing and lifelong education. In some education systems, especially those of developing countries, the realisation of this concept would necessitate the restructuring and reform of higher education, in order to eliminate bottlenecks, and establish lateral and vertical channels among the various fields and levels of educational and training offerings, to promote occupational and educational mobility and, consequently social mobility.

In general, therefore, higher education should be linked with the abilities and performance standards of the learner, irrespective of the type or stream of pre-university education or training he experienced. Furthermore, the status of vocational education can be enhanced in practice through the establishment of a comprehensive and diversified network of non-formal and adult educational and training facilities and services which are accessible to the employed, as well as to the unemployed, to enable them move along and up the educational and professional ladder at any point or stage of their careers; thus fostering their personal development, enhancing their occupational and social mobility, and upgrading the quality and productivity of work sites.

In most developing countries, such facilities and services suffer from two main shortcomings. First, they fall short of the minimum requirements needed to have an impact in such aspects as quantity, quality, geographical coverage, flexibility and accessibility. Secondly, such facilities and services seem to be utilised more by those who are already better educated and who can afford the costs involved. Thus, instead of acting as a means to compensate for earlier inequalities in educational and training opportunities, and as a vehicle to contribute to bridging the social and economic gap between the various groups of society, adult education facilities and services face the risk, in most developing countries, of widening the educational, occupational and social gap between the privileged and the underprivileged, between the haves and the have-nots. Other aspects of the status issue of vocational education include such factors as the status of the vocational teacher, the gender issue, and the vocationalisation of general education.

It is not unusual in many education and training systems to find that vocational teachers are not of equal status, socially and economically, to their general education counterparts. It is also not unusual to find that the relevant vocational education facilities and services are structured basically around the needs of male learners, with the result that the role of females as learners, instructors, planners and providers of services, lags considerably behind the role of males. Finally, a great service can be offered to the status issue, if a strong element of vocational education, or more specifically prevocational education, is incorporated as part of general education in the form diversified practical activities and life experiences, derived from the various socio-economic sectors.

ECONOMICS OF VOCATIONAL EDUCATION

Three major factors have to be explored when the economics of vocational education systems are discussed. The first factor is concerned with the sources of finance and methods of funding; while the second factor is concerned with such matters as costs, efficiency and effectiveness, and hence with the socio-economic return on investment in vocational education. The third factor caters for the evaluation and assessment of the relevant systems and programmes. The sources of finance and methods of funding of vocational education programmes vary considerably. Nevertheless, two such sources predominate: the first represents the taxpayers through central and/or local budgets, while the second source represents employers in industry and business, who are the main beneficiaries of the output of vocational education systems.

Other sources with less impact include learners and trainees themselves and their families, in the case of fee-paying programmes; income generating activities; grants and donations, especially for such programmes as those directed to special groups, including the handicapped and the underprivileged. In most developing countries, public sources of finance for vocational education usually predominate. Public funding is in general utilised to finance school systems, and suffers usually from being inadequate, especially in countries with limited resources, where vocational education is not considered a priority in national budgets.

A dynamic multifaceted approach to the funding issue, with the objective of diversifying sources of finance, should be adopted in developing countries to ensure adequacy and sustainability of funding. Such an approach has yet to gain recognition and feasibility in such countries. Matters related to cost, efficiency and effectiveness of vocational education schemes, which represent the second factor concerning the economics of such schemes, pose a big challenge in most developing countries. The relevant issues here include, on the planning or macro level, system choice or the school vs. the enterprise issue, the broad vs. the narrow base approach to the area of specialisation, and the duration of the vocational education programme. On the operational or micro level, such issues include trainee-instructor ratios, utilisation factors of training facilities, choice of equipment and technologies, and size and nature of productive activities.

Evaluation systems and techniques, which represent the third factor concerning the economics of vocational education, are far from being common practice in developing countries. To be effective, evaluation systems should incorporate three main elements:

i) *Internal evaluation*: Internal evaluation, which is mainly concerned with assessing the degree of compatibility between the outputs of the vocational education programme and the performance objectives specified for such programmes.

ii) *Economic evaluation*: Economic evaluation, which is basically concerned with such indicators as cost-benefit criteria, changes in learner's income, changes in productivity at the workplace, comparative costing of different vocational education systems, and optimum utilisation of training facilities and services.

iii) *External evaluation*: External evaluation, which is generally concerned with assessing the degree of computability between the outputs of the vocational education programmes on the one hand, and labour market needs and employment requirements, on the other.

In developing countries, all aspects related to the economics of vocational education are sources of concern, and even frustration, especially when taking into consideration the relatively high cost of vocational education programmes, compared with other educational offerings.

REGIONAL AND INTERNATIONAL DIMENSIONS OF VOCATIONAL EDUCATION

The approach to issues related to human resources development in general, and vocational education in particular, is no more a purely national concern. For sometime now, it has been a regional concern; and now it is even becoming a concern with international dimensions that should take into consideration emerging conditions of increasingly globalised economies of the world, manifested by the changing structure and framework of world trade, labour mobility, common markets, commodity standards, multinationals, and the geographical characteristics of industrialisation.

The economies of developed Western countries, as an example, are shifting away from the manufacturing sector to the services sector, with much of the manufacturing activities moving to less developed countries in Asia and Latin America, attracted by reduced production costs. It is thus becoming increasingly essential to think regionally and even globally when planning, defining policies and designing programmes at the national level, for the quantitative and qualitative aspects of vocational education as a component of human resources development, especially in such matters as job classification, skill standards, educational levels, information systems and the identification of training needs.

We talk freely of the regional and international dimensions of vocational education at the macro level, but we seem to be timid and shy in the face of some of the issues at the micro level. Take, for example, the two concepts of vocational education and vocational training. We frequently come across, or use, these two terms, sometimes to mean different things and sometimes to mean the same thing.

The split and schism between Vocational Education and Vocational Training is believed to be artificial in modern vocational schemes and programmes. The fact that the split still exists is due probably to past prejudices and administrative structures. So, nothing short of the full integration of the implications and contents of the two terms is acceptable now. The split might have been justified decades ago when it was usual for workers to acquire the skills needed for their jobs purely through traditional time-serving informal apprenticeship schemes, consisting predominantly of on-the-job practical experiences.

Jobs are classified according to two main variables: the field of specialisation and the occupational level. The content of any vocational preparation programme for a job is analysed into its constituent functions, duties and skills, specifying the theoretical content and knowledge needed. Thus the needs and requirements of the job dictate the structure and content of the vocational programme, whether it is called vocational education or vocational training.

The fact that the vocational programme is implemented in an educational institution or within a work environment in an enterprise should not affect the basic structure and content of the programme, simply because the needs and requirements of the job are independent of the venue that is utilised for the implementation of the preparation programme.

The schism between Vocational Education and Vocational Training can be ended, and the barriers demolished if vocational programmes are structured around the needs of the job and the needs of the learner, irrespective of the venue of implementation, or the agency responsible for its financing or administration. The two most renowned international agencies in the field of vocational education and training, UNESCO and ILO, need to address this issue seriously, so that we stop talking different things about what should be the same thing, and stop insisting that UNESCO's role is vocational education, while ILO's role is vocational training.

It is worthwhile mentioning here in this context that, because UNESCO and ILO communicate with member countries through different channels and national agencies, two systems of human power preparation at the basic occupational levels emerge sometimes side by side with little or no coordination, and sometimes with rivalry and mistrust. In short, the regional and global dimensions of vocational education cannot be properly explored without investigating their cultural reflections and outreaches, especially that globalisation is a trend that is permeating all aspects of life: economic, social and cultural.

This would obviously present another challenge to planners of vocational education systems, and would justify more the broad-based human approach to vocational education programmes to complement the professional and specialised approach. What is really needed in our education systems is, more and more, the liberalisation of vocational education and the vocationalisation of general education.

INFLUENCE OF GLOBALISATION ON TECHNICAL AND VOCATIONAL EDUCATION

Information Technology (IT) is at the root of a process of transformation in the course of which industrialised societies are changing into knowledge societies and the management of production into the management of knowledge. There will be less and less manual work while computers become the main tools catering for the information needs of all professions. As a result, letters and figures, into which all procedures have to be translated, become more and more important for all human activities at work and in private life.

The end of the division of the world has opened the borders to the free flow of capital, goods and information and to the unhindered travel of people at large, but not yet in all parts of the world. Going global is the challenge to entrepreneurs and, of course, to their employees. As an example, cross-border activities in a united Europe demand the same competencies in all participating countries, i.e., language and more knowledge about partner countries, their economy, culture and their legal and social systems. Growing ecological consciousness will become a very important economic factor in the foreseeable future.

Eco-knowledge is an important part of it, but eco-thinking is even more important. It has to be part of all education, general and vocational. Curriculum revisions, new syllabuses or educational reforms cannot master all these changes. What we need are new ways of thinking. To master the changes in thinking about the needs of our world seems to me the most difficult task of education.

As the value imperative to remain competitive has become more demanding, so there has been a corresponding increase in the capability expectations of the workforce. There is a point in this development where a new balance in responsibility in the partnership between management and the workforce now tilts more towards the workforce than prevailed in the past. This is not the result of a power struggle but the consequence of inevitable changes in the organisation of work.

In several European countries these changes are also reflected in government policies and ultimately in what is expected of VET. Tripartite bodies are responsible for VET-Standard development and implementation in many countries of the world. Thus, the ability of employers and trade unions to describe rather exactly what their needs are concerning the role and the competence profile of future skilled workers and employees has been developed and improved. The communication between the world of work and the world of education, which very often seems to be non-existent, has grown into a new culture within research institutes or employment offices where these tripartite bodies meet regularly.

One of the most dangerous consequences of fundamental changes now prevailing in politics and, of course, in education is uncertainty, and following this, anxiety. In Eastern Europe, where nearly all established frameworks and structures have fallen apart, uncertainty and anxiety are probably the prime reasons for the failure of leadership, but also in Western industrialised countries on their way into knowledge societies, some of them with particularly high unemployment rates, as well as in Asian countries which are shaken by a threatening economic crisis or in Africa and South-America, uncertainty and anxiety are well-known companions for a majority of people. Therefore, it is one of the most important tasks of education to enable people to cope successfully with uncertainty through:

i) information and knowledge about the reasons for the changes, including systems' knowledge (e.g., computer systems, banking systems, free-market systems);

ii) skills on how to gather and select information and knowledge, and how to use them in planning and decision-making processes;
iii) problem-solving and practical skills, social and team skills;
iv) entrepreneurial skills; and
v) The development of the learner's personality through general, vocational and professional education.

If education shall act successfully in this very important field, educators need the help of the whole society, not only parents. The corporate world and the trade unions have a responsibility for cooperation with the world of education for their own sake. A main task of education, including vocational education and training, must surely be to maintain the freedom to hold diverse opinions regardless of political, religious and philosophical boundaries.

In the information driven world of work:

i) computers are the common tool for managers as well as for front line workers;
ii) all information is being digitised and transformed into computer-compatible letters and figures;
iii) the internet is established as a worldwide information web, using English as the *lingua franca* of the knowledge age.

As a consequence, mathematics, one's own language and English are becoming more important for vocational education and training than many of the practical skills that have traditionally been related to specialised training. Initial vocational education and training pursue in their turn the kind of educational objectives that have traditionally been the prerogative of general education. They include:

i) *learning to learn* (on the job; integrating theory with practice; learning by reviewing practice; applying learning methods in practice; developing social capabilities that cannot be taught); and

ii) *becoming a mature and responsible contributor* (acquiring overarching capabilities like acting in a group, thinking in process terms, taking responsibility for others and for one's own achievement).

The traditional boundaries between general and vocational education on the one hand and education and training on the other have become obstacles to learning for real life. There is no one-way-road of learning transfer from the so-called industrialised countries to the so-called developing world. Those who believe that they already know the problems of tomorrow have already lost the learning competition.

There is a widely shared consensus about the goals of education. It is to prepare young people for life by developing their intellect, their aptitudes and their talents; and to create opportunities for them to reach their full potential. But education should also enable them to earn their own living and take part in the democratic process. All educational systems have to serve these purposes. Vocational education, i.e., the education and training of skilled workers and employees, has to be broader and more diversified. Take for example:

i) *a car mechanic* must have diagnostic skills and knowledge (computer literacy), be customer-oriented (direct personal contact), have all the skills of the trade (high tech), must take into account the ecological effects of his work, be able to calculate the cost of a repair and, more generally, be conscious of adding value;

ii) *a farmer or horticulturist* must be knowledgeable in biology, chemistry, management, marketing, engineering (mechanical) and have customer orientation; he must be able to find and exploit niches in the market;

iii) *a worker in one of the growing service industries,* e.g., in the tourist, hospitality or leisure industry can be a well educated and trained leisure manager with a broad cultural background and communication skills; and

iv) *a health care assistant* in one of the broadest fields of services where people of all ages can perform full time or part-time services once they have access to adequate education and training.

The key to success in vocational education is to create learning opportunities through which people can develop their ability to learn autonomously and use what they have learned to make a difference in their workplace. All new learning activities following this new paradigm have one characteristic in common: the learner steps into the centre of the learning process, gathers information and, as far as possible, acts independently. The teacher/trainer also changes his role to become coach, advisor and tutor.

CHALLENGES IN THE TWENTY-FIRST CENTURY AND FUTURE STRATEGIES

The trends of globalisation of trade and labour markets, rapidly changing technologies, and mass unemployment resulting from the recent economic crisis, are expected to continue in the twenty-first century. This trend will foster rapidly paced changes in future industrial structures and employment patterns. The effect on and changes in the labour market are that some jobs are declining in significance, others growing in importance and others still require completely new or different skills. The size of the workforce employed in the service and technology industries, where a high-level education and skills are required, will increase; while the demand for low-skilled workers will shrink.

Many employees are likely to change jobs, and possibly even careers, several times during their working lives. The changing nature of labour market trends has significant implications for education, implying *inter alia* the need to provide lifelong learning, continuing and recurrent technical and vocational education, and continued upgrading of knowledge and skills. In an effort to respond to the emerging challenges in the twenty-first century, the government will continue to implement current reforms.

The following are measures and policy recommendations to be considered:

i) The common school curriculum should be revised to emphasise basic education rather than specialised education. Core competencies required for students should be identified and integrated into the Basic Common Curriculum from the first to the tenth grade, as proposed in the Seventh Curriculum which will be effective from the year 2000. Constant improvements in the area of knowledge and skills prove imperative for the future workforce to acquire the basis for developing further knowledge and skills as quickly and effectively as possible. This demands an adequate general knowledge level in order to facilitate the development of knowledge in related areas, that is, a core of "generic knowledge".

ii) Integration of the senior secondary school curriculum. Senior secondary schools willing to do so can integrate and manage the curricula of both vocational and general schools in order to enable students to choose from a wide selection of courses during the second and third year. This will enable students to satisfy requirements for further education while at the same time acquiring work-related knowledge and skills that will help them to enter the workforce. Schools that integrate and manage both curricula will minimise the number of compulsory courses which students must take and will increase the number of elective subjects.

iii) Lifelong education at different levels should be expanded to benefit each and every citizen. The educational trend has shifted so that more and more students are opting to undertake further study beyond that of senior secondary school. Higher education institutes such as polytechnic universities, polytechnic colleges and junior colleges should therefore be strengthened and equipped as lifelong educational institutions allowing people of all ages to receive further occupational education. Flexible access to vocational education and training throughout life should be ensured.

iv) A School-To-Work Transition (STWT) system must be developed. STWT should begin in the earliest years of schooling, combining efforts in educational improvement, workforce development and economic development. The goal of STWT is to smooth the transition process for all students, including college-bound and non-college-bound youth, disadvantaged youth and out-of-school youth. The system seeks to find a balance in preparing students for "real jobs" without limiting their employment and school opportunities. The components of the system are:

   a) work-based learning;
   b) school-based learning;
   c) connecting activities which articulate between the school based and work-based components; and
   d) career-awareness programmes.

v) Enterprise training should be encouraged. Companies, particularly those which invested in technology-intensive industries, require a continuous updating of skills and knowledge for which formal schools are inadequately prepared. Companies provide the best setting for workers to acquire the work-related knowledge and skills necessary to absorb future technology speedily. Enterprises have to become "places of learning" in addition to being places of work. Training policies should encourage enterprises to provide further training of their employees.

The world is moving towards an information-based economy where the effectiveness of an enterprise or a country is determined by the quality of its products and services. Production systems based on new technologies that enable greater productivity and flexibility demand that all workers constantly must update their skills and become more entrepreneurial. The evidence clearly shows that the most productive nations are those characterised by a flexible and well-qualified labour market, one with a rich and diverse mix of skills which are continuously updated and developed throughout life.

Technical and vocational education and training (TVET) is most directly concerned with the acquisition of the knowledge and skills required for the world of work, formal and informal, urban and rural. And every country must adapt its TVET programme to cater to the skill requirements of its workplace of the twenty-first century. We have seen that these skills requirements may vary considerably according to the stage of socio-economic development of each country.

Nevertheless, it has been clearly demonstrated that every country, regardless of its state of development, is compelled to redesign its national TVET programme if it is to address effectively the employment and development issues of the twenty-first century.

In Asia, the economic situation can change dramatically suddenly, creating massive problems of unemployment and forcing many young people to opt for self-employment in the future. Thus the need to develop more coherent education, training and employment policies, and to find ways to co-ordinate the work of Ministers of Education, Labour and Social Welfare.

Yet again, a major international forum has stressed that the current international developmental paradigm cannot continue indefinitely because of its adverse impact on the environment, on education and the social sector. A sustainable development paradigm must be arrived at and that the TVET of the future must not only prepare individuals for employment in the information society, but also make them responsible citizens who give due consideration to preserving the integrity of their environment and the welfare of others.

Integral Component of Lifelong Learning

In an era characterised by the challenge of globalisation, rapid technological changes and economic uncertainty, it is imperative that all stakeholders work together to develop legislation and policies, establish institutional structures and redesign curricula to ensure that TVET caters adequately to the varied needs of all members of society to enter and re-enter the world of work. For this purpose, continuous TVET opportunities should be provided for achieving both personal and social development. UNESCO's activities therefore should aim at:

i) Including vocational subjects in general education curricula to facilitate the young generation to obtain generic technological knowledge and key pre-vocational skills—making TVET for all an integral part of the national educational policy;

ii) Developing the articulation between technical and vocational education on the one hand, and other sectors of education on the other, emphasising the recognition of prior learning and work experience, and raising the status of TVET in education systems;

iii) Promoting coordination between formal education and informal training systems, ministries responsible for education, training, labour and social welfare;

iv) Fostering the involvement of all stakeholders, particularly private sectors, in the provision of TVETE and improving the link and cooperation with the world of work.

TVET can play an instrumental role in developing a new generation of individuals who will face the challenge of achieving sustainable socioeconomic development. A number of new subjects (issues) therefore need to be incorporated into

TVET teaching and learning or be further emphasised for the sake of the future of all of us as we struggle to learn throughout life. A well-trained technical workforce is essential for any country's efforts to achieve sustainable development. Thus, UNESCO's activities should aim at:

i) Ensuring that TVET is an integral part of every nation's development agenda, and a valued and integral part of its education and human resource development strategy;
ii) Including environmental issues in all TVET curricula with the objective of promoting the concept of sustainable development;
iii) Emphasising the acquisition of entrepreneurial skills, creativity, team and communication skills as part of TVET;
iv) Introducing and applying the new information and communication technologies in the TVET teaching and learning process without losing valuable aspects of traditional teaching methods;
v) Paying special attention to providing training for the tourism and hospitality industries which are a potential avenue towards employment creation and economic growth in the developing world.

Besides preparing people for the world of work, TVET is also expected to be an instrument for social cohesion and integration. The general access to and availability of TVET and the right to work are closely inter-linked issues. UNESCO will therefore assist member states in their efforts to make TVET programmes comprehensive and adequately inclusive in order to accommodate the needs of all learners. UNESCO's activities in this respect should aim at:

i) Promoting special initiatives and efforts to ensure equal access to TVET for girls and women, and to eliminate the very strong historic gender basis against women which has for too long characterised TVET policy and practice;

ii) Making TVET programmes, both formal and informal, available to the unemployed and various marginalised groups including early school leavers, the disabled, the rural poor, displaced persons and demobilised solders in post-conflict situations, contributing to the UN effort to alleviate poverty;

iii) Re-orienting vocational guidance and counselling to reach out to all members of society;

iv) Promoting flexible access to lifelong learning and training.

To meet the major challenges posed by the requirement for human resources development, UNESCO's Member States have petitioned the Organisation to upgrade its activities in TVET, and to provide them with more effective assistance in this field. UNESCO launched an International Programme on Technical and Vocational Education from the beginning of the 2000-2001 biennium to meet such a demand. The following is a proposed framework of this Programme. The Programme actions will be designed and implemented through the following modalities:

Improving member states' policy-making capacity

The following actions will be planned to assist member states' efforts in formulating relevant policies for the development of TVET as a component of national development agenda:

i) Providing national decision makers with comparative and analytical information on national policies for reforming TVET systems, best practices of TVET delivery models and research findings in various member states;

ii) Conducting international, regional and sub-regional meetings for policy makers, professionals and researchers to exchange views, experiences, TVET curricula and teaching packages and ideas;

iii) Identifying the factors that determine the quality and pertinence of TVET with a view to improving its status and attractiveness in education systems;

iv) In co-operation with member states, rationalising and refining the collection of national statistics relating to TVET and developing indicators to facilitate decision making, planning and assessment at the national and international level;

v) Providing information and assistance to member states on formulating the national legislative framework for TVET.

Assisting member states' institutional capacity building

The following actions will be planned to strengthen TVET institutions' capacities in research, development and training:

i) Supporting regional activities and providing guidelines to member states on the preparation of TVET teaching and training personnel;

ii) Assisting member states in using information/ communication technologies as a tool for teaching and learning both in direct contact and in distance learning mode;

iii) Compiling an annotated inventory of existing methodologies, instruments and tools for the development of TVET systems and various delivery patterns;

iv) Implementing projects for developing sample modular materials and interactive learning packages for internet and intranet use.

Enhancing international cooperation

Actions to promote international cooperation in TVET will emphasise North-South and South-South exchanges, as well as cooperation among countries with similar problems. This will also include efforts to strengthen the capacity for international communication of UNEVOC centres in less privileged communication environments, particularly in the least developed countries, in small states and in some parts of Africa:

i) Collecting and disseminating information on curricular competencies in order to enhance the uniformity and portability of vocational skills, competencies and credentials among countries and regions;

ii) Strengthening the existing UNEVOC network and improving the capacity of national UNEVOC centres as both centres of information and action;

iii) Establishing close cooperation with other UN agencies, donor agencies, development banks and NGOs active in TVET, generating an alliance (as for EFA) in support of TVET and the new vision generated by the Seoul Congress;

iv) Advocacy in support of TVET as an integral part of the development agenda of bilateral and multilateral donors and financial institutions, promoting debt swaps and debt relief for education and training and respect for national human development priorities;

v) Matchmaking among national projects, donor agencies and relevant NGOs;

vi) Initiating international events that would draw public attention to TVET.

UNESCO will seek to forge an international alliance in support of TVET. In particular, we expect to forge a common policy with the ILO for the joint development and execution of policies and programmes aimed at the alleviation of poverty and the strengthening of links among education, training and employment, but drawing in other partners such as the World Bank, the European Training Foundation, SEAMEO, KRIVET, CINTERFOR, to name a few.

UNESCO with the help of several key bilateral donors, partners like KRIVET and UNEVOC Centres in Australia, Greece, Brazil, Korea, United Arab Emirates and elsewhere will support its UNEVOC Network and will provide tangible support to its 190 national centres, sponsoring fellowships and exchanges aimed at promoting national capacity-building and international cooperation for the renewal of TVET.

The overall planning and monitoring of UNESCO's long-term Programme on Technical and Vocational Education will be the responsibility of the Secretariat at UNESCO Headquarters, and will promote cooperation with other international partners. Particular attention will be paid to enhancing cooperation and promoting activities at regional and sub-regional levels. The major UNESCO field offices in Bangkok, Beirut, Dakar and Santiago and the regional networks of educational innovation for development shall continue to play the key role in the implementation of the recommendations of the Seoul Congress.

UNESCO, with the collaboration of ILO, will launch a one-stop website on the internet dedicated to supporting TVET, to be known as the "TVET Implementation Centre". It will place online critical information and guidelines, examples of best practices, etc., with guided search and assist features, to cater for users of different levels in member states. It will carry extensive references and links to resources at other sites, generating greater development and use of these. This "implementation tool" will increase the efficacy of missions and consultancies, which must continue.

With a generous offer made by the Government of Germany, the establishment of an International Centre for Technical and Vocational Education in Bonn has been proposed. This Centre is expected to be the technical backbone supporting the international UNEVOC network and strengthening the capacity of national UNEVOC centres by providing (a) clearing-house service, i.e., providing information, conducting research and studies; and (b) training of personnel from national UNEVOC centres.

Within the framework of this international network, a number of regional centres shall be established with UNESCO's support, in order to facilitate the networking and programme activities implemented at the regional and/or sub-regional levels. Several member states (including Australia, Brazil, Pakistan, Republic of Korea, the Russian Federation, etc) have already proposed to host such regional centres. In accordance with the specific strengths of these centres, they may also assume the functions of Centres of Excellence in given field such as the application of new information/communication technology in TVET.

While UNESCO is the leading agency in the United Nations System in the field of education, many other intergovernmental and non-governmental agencies also deal with various aspects of education and training. In planning and implementing its Programme on Technical and Vocational Education, UNESCO will seek to develop close cooperation with other partners giving the Programme an interagency character.

REFERENCES

Hallak, J., "Investing in the future: setting educational priorities in the developing world", *Paris: UNESCO/IIEP*; Oxford: Pergamon Press, 1990.

Hegelheimer, A., *Financing of vocational training*, German Foundation for International Development (DSE), 1986.

Lauglo, J., "Vocational training and the banker's faith in the private sector", *Comparative Education Review,* Vol. 36, No. 2, 1992.

Munbodh, S., "The management of industrial and vocational training: the experience of the Industrial and Vocational Training Board (Mauritius)", paper submitted at the IIEP/Prg.BS/95, Paris, 8 June 1995.

UNESCO, "Convention on technical and vocational education", *adopted by the General Conference at its twenty-fifth session*, 10 November, Paris, 1989.

Wilson, D., "The effectiveness of national training boards", *Training discussion paper no.110, Geneva,* Training Policies Branch, ILO, 1993.

World Bank, "Vocational and technical education and training", *A World Bank Policy Paper*, Washington, D.C.: World Bank, 1991.

3

TVE: Towards a New Vision

We have considered the emerging challenges of the twenty-first century, a century that will be an era of knowledge, information and communication. Globalisation and the revolution in information and communication technology have signalled the need for a new human-centred development paradigm. The Technical and Vocational Education (TVE), as an integral component of lifelong learning, has a crucial role to play in this new era as an effective tool to realise the objectives of a culture of peace, environmentally sound sustainable development, social cohesion, and international citizenship.

Mindful of the opportunities that lie ahead of us and those which will progressively unfold, and cognizant of the policies, partnerships and resources needed to raise the status and broaden the traditional vision of TVE, we need to recognise the need for strengthened international partnerships particularly, to address the needs of developing countries.

The twenty-first century will bring a radically different economy and society with profound implications for technical and vocational education. TVE systems must adapt to these key features which include globalisation, an ever-changing technological scenario, the revolution in information and communications, and the consequent rapid pace of social change. The implications of these transformations include the increased mobility of labour and capital, uneven impacts upon rich and poor, and emerging market economies in both rural and industrial sectors. The knowledge-based society which these changes are bringing offers exciting new modalities for education and training. These social and economic trends predicate the need for a new development paradigm which holds a culture of peace and environmentally sound sustainable development as its central features.

Accordingly the values, attitudes, policies and practices of TVE must have their foundations in this paradigm which will encompass inclusiveness and wider access, a shift to human development needs, and empowerment for effective participation in the world of work. Its focus must be on the needs and potential of the individual in society. TVE has a crucial role to play in this new paradigm by providing skills for all and should include the poor, the excluded and the unreached so that education remains an accessible basic human right. The universalisation of TVE and the learning skill it imparts would enhance access to education for all citizens of the world. A new holistic approach is required so that education for the twenty-first century will include all domains of learning incorporating general and vocational education to enable the learner of the twenty-first century to launch into a lifelong continuum of knowledge, values and attitudes, and competencies and skills.

The ultimate goal of such an approach would be the creation of a learning society. Therefore TVE systems must be reformed to give life to this new paradigm by achieving flexibility, innovation and productivity, imparting the skills required, addressing the implications of changing labour markets, training and retraining the employed, unemployed and the marginalised with the objective of achieving equality of opportunity for all in both the formal and the informal sectors of the economy. There must be a new partnership between education and the world of work to address the need to develop a synergy between the sectors of education and industry and the various other economic sectors, to foster the development of generic competencies, the work ethic, technological and entrepreneurial skills, and for imparting human values and standards for responsible citizenship.

There is a need to introduce the required changes in a manner suitable for each country, so as to empower and engage human beings in the context of the new paradigm, with TVE as a common key focus of the reform process. The prerequisites of the TVE response to the new paradigm include appropriate societal values and attitudes, embracing the new technologies, making new policy and financial commitments, and taking account local, regional, and global opportunities and concerns. The sheer magnitude of the trends of the twenty-first century demands a political commitment and bold policy responses which are both regional and international.

Education and Training throughout Life

Lifelong learning is a journey with many pathways and TVE is an integral part of the voyage. Therefore TVE systems should be designed as developmental life experiences with cultural and environmental aspects in addition to their economic dimensions. To make the maximum contribution to lifelong learning TVE systems need to be open, flexible and learner-oriented. They must do more than just provide the learner with knowledge and skills for specific jobs. They must also prepare individuals more generally for life and the world of work.

TVE is for personal, social and economic benefit. TVE needs to be based on a learning culture shared by individuals, industry, different economic sectors and government in which individuals are empowered to take progressively more responsibility for their own knowledge-management and independent learning while public and private providers ensure programmes that facilitate access to and through the pathways of lifelong learning. TVE has an important role in reducing levels of anxiety in the midst of constant uncertainty by providing information and knowledge, skills and competencies, entrepreneurial capacity and the development of the human personality. All nations require a coherent education policy and coordinated education systems within which TVE must be a fundamental part.

TVE should develop close interfaces with all other education sectors, particularly schools and universities, to facilitate seamless pathways for learners. The emphasis must be on articulation, accreditation and recognition of prior learning to enhance their opportunities. Within this spectrum TVE has a responsibility to ensure a sound initial education and training aimed at learning to learn, the most precious skill for all citizens both young and adult. Perhaps the biggest challenge which faces TVE is to coordinate the needs of a general and a vocational education through curriculum, pedagogy and delivery.

Each country will wish to pursue its preferred approach to coordinate these domains but it is clear that the demands of the twenty-first century require new synergies between these fundamental pillars of education and training systems. TVE should inspire in young people a positive attitude to innovation, enable them to help shape change and prepare them for self-reliance and citizenship. TVE is particularly important in ensuring a seamless transition from the school to the workplace. To achieve this it needs an holistic approach which captures the dichotomies of the academic and the vocational, the theory and the applied, knowing and doing, the use of the head and the hand. This requires effective partnerships with schools and with industry and other economic sectors which embrace shared values, shared curriculum, shared resources, and shared outcomes. The informal economic sector is often excluded in the spectrum of lifelong learning.

TVE has a vital role to play in reaching out to this sector in every way possible to ensure that the less privileged have access to the pathways of continuous learning. This applies with equal force to those who drop out of the formal cycle of education. To achieve all of these aspirations for Technical and Vocational Education a number of urgent considerations must be addressed:

i) the status and prestige of TVE must be enhanced in the eyes of the community and the media. This includes raising the status of teachers in TVE systems through attention to their own skills and competencies and the provision of resources for their task. It will also require strong marketing of the capabilities of TVE to its many stakeholders, accompanied by a simplification of TVE in the minds of many who find its language, its products and its modalities too complex. Publicising and disseminating models of good practice in TVE are also important. There is a need to promote parity of esteem between vocational and general education, especially in developing countries;

ii) the sectors of education must achieve more effective interrelationships to facilitate more seamless pathways for learners. They do not need to be homogenised; each sector can retain its identity and they all can recognise each other's passports and visas at their borders;

iii) there must be flexibility in programme administration and curriculum design to facilitate a smooth passage through lifelong learning and provide continuous entry, exit and re-entry points;

iv) career guidance and counselling is of the utmost importance for all clients of the education and training systems and needs to be significantly strengthened;

v) Career guidance should take into account the needs of industry, the individual and the family and be sensitive to each learner's requirements and circumstances. Its role should be extended to prepare students and adults for the real possibility of frequent career change which could include periods of unemployment and employment in the informal sector;

vi) all stakeholders, particularly industry and educationalists, must be involved in new TVE partnerships. Each has much to learn from the other in approaches to lifelong learning;

vii) the high cost of many TVE programmes must be addressed. They should be redesigned to incorporate more workplace learning;

viii) the lifelong learning continuum will be best sustained if there is a diversity of funding, a diversity of providers, and a diversity of delivery mechanisms. Innovative approaches to flexible delivery of TVE including the use of information and communication technology and distance learning should be particularly welcomed;

ix) quality assurance is essential to ensure a new higher status for TVE. Qualification standards, certification processes, valid assessment methods and acceptable outcomes are all key ingredients and should be the hallmarks of all TVE systems;

x) We need to understand more about the critical moments of choice on the journey of lifelong learning. More research should be encouraged to help understand the key issues, dilemmas, potential barriers and opportunities which confront the voyager at the various phases of the journey.

Flexible Access to TVE throughout Life

TVE programmes are often de-linked from the production process and to a large extent are delivered using traditional theoretical methods. TVE does not address the needs of the informal sector where most production activities go on. The assurance of quality programmes and the award of various forms of certification is another major challenge for TVE.

There is a proliferation of certificates and diplomas ranging from short-term courses (days and weeks) to long-term (months and years). This is often difficult for employers to determine the worth of such credentialing resulting in underemployment in some cases. There is a need for clear government policies that give priority to TVE by allocating appropriate funds for its execution. Partnerships between TVE institutions and enterprises will foster better working relationships that will support and strengthen TVE programmes. This will also give the TVE teachers and trainers opportunities to update their experiences. There is a need to find alternative methods of delivery of instruction for TVE. Teaching institutions and teachers should be reoriented to use flexible teaching and learning materials. Some of these should include: the development of modularised curricula and assessment methods; the development and use of appropriate technologies for instruction—online services and training materials, computerised learning packages, use of CD-ROMs, intranet and internet, etc.

INNOVATING THE EDUCATION AND TRAINING PROCESS

The challenges facing the learner of the twenty-first century demand innovative approaches in TVE. This is seen most clearly in the need for a re-oriented curriculum to take account of new subjects and issues of importance. Obvious examples would include technology, environment, understanding of foreign languages and cultures, entrepreneurial capacity and requirements of the rapidly growing service industries connected with leisure, tourism and hospitality. The rapid pace of change also introduces the prospect of a virtual curriculum whereby learners must be prepared to cope with the obsolescence of their knowledge and skills, and the introduction of new elements which have yet to appear in common usage.

They must also be prepared for a radically new labour market in which traditional wage-employment may be the experience of only a minority and self-employment in various forms may offer a high potential for economic independence in a new era of entrepreneurship. The new information technology has opened up a whole new potential in technology-based learning. It should be possible to use and apply simple as well as modern technology and the new information and communication technologies in the TVE teaching and learning process without losing the valuable aspects of traditional teaching methods, particularly the personal nature of the teacher-learner relationship.

Technology-based learning should play a crucial role in the development of a culture of lifelong learning with the capacity to empower learners by providing them with multiple new pathways to meet their education and training needs. The new technologies must be harnessed to provide widespread access to TVE. They should be used to make distance irrelevant and to render curriculum-based knowledge and vocational guidance information more easily accessible to all. They have the potential to offer flexibility in time and location to TVE delivery, and should enable TVE to function as a catalyst for the penetration of new technologies in underdeveloped regions of the world, particularly in rural areas.

As the workplace calls for more sophisticated skills, a sound basic education must be provided as a prerequisite foundation for TVE. This should involve the acquisition of more complex competencies in school, including enhanced literary and numeracy skills and the ability to understand and communicate through the tools of modern technology.

Since technology comes at a price, ways must be found through partnerships with industry, financial and aid agencies, regional and international cooperation, to address the high costs involved, especially for developing countries. New ways must also be found to share intellectual property for the benefit of learners in all countries and situations. Given the essential need for innovation in TVE, the role of the teacher remains paramount. New methods must be found for the initial training of teachers accompanied by the continuous upgrading of their competencies and professional development. A rethinking must take place as to the qualifications required of the TVE teacher of the twenty-first century, including the optimum balance of training acquired on the campus and in the workplace. They must be assisted to develop new and appropriate instruments of assessment, accreditation, articulation and certification standards.

TVE needs an early global warning system and more futuristic studies to enable preparation for changes in the work place and in society. Industry must be involved with governments and research centres in identifying the knowledge, skills and competencies which will be required by the changing economy so that TVE systems can adapt. The prospect of competencies applicable across regions and internationally should be addressed to respond to the projected escalation in resource mobility in the next century.

Current TVE teacher training was identified as problematic because university staff need improved training themselves and industry experience. It was agreed that TVE teacher training needs to be given the same recognition as teachers in general and higher education and that TVE teacher training needs to be continuous/lifelong learning. A key reason for the drift of TVE teachers to industry was seen to be that they are not valued sufficiently, reflected in salary scales, and they can attract higher pay in industry and are therefore lost to TVE. UNESCO should support the development and conduct of professional development programmes for TVE teachers in the development of flexible learning materials and facilitate the mutual exchange of experiences through the UNEVOC network.

TVE curriculum development encompassing environmental issues needs immediate attention since environmental concerns are urgent. Strategies may include the introduction of environmental issues and appropriate foreign languages into curriculum using an integrated approach to ensure that environmental issues are not treated as add-on courses.

TECHNICAL AND VOCATIONAL EDUCATION FOR ALL

TVE is one of the most powerful instruments for enabling all members of the community to face new challenges and to find their roles as productive members of society. It is an effective tool for achieving social cohesion, integration and self-esteem. TVE programmes should be designed as comprehensive and inclusive systems to accommodate the needs of all learners; they must be accessible to all. Special efforts are needed to reach previously marginalised groups. Where specialised programmes are required, these should be designed to facilitate entry into the mainstream, thus ensuring continued access to lifelong learning.

TVE programmes, both formal and non-formal, must be made available in varying modes of accessible delivery, to the unemployed, early school leavers, out of school youth, those disadvantaged by distance and location, rural populations, indigenous people, those in the midst of urban despair, populations engaged in informal labour markets with poor working and living circumstances, children working under hazardous conditions, refugees, migrants, and demobilised soldiers in post-conflict situations.

The under-representation of women in TVE is of particular concern. Traditional perceptions of appropriate roles for men and women in the workplace should be challenged. TVE must respond with gender-inclusive learning programmes, both in content and delivery, including measures to attract men into previously female-dominated training and careers. Faculty need to be gender-sensitive. For the promotion of equal access of girls and women to TVE courses, more effective forms of educational and vocational guidance and counselling must be provided, along with gender-sensitive guidance and counselling materials.

At the same time the learning and working environments must be made more suitable for the participation of girls and women, overt and covert bias and discrimination must be removed, and a positive image and appropriate incentives for female participation in TVE should be created. To overcome the lack of employment opportunities for girls and women, and the misconception that they are incapable of performing particular tasks, TVE programmes emphasising the development of their entrepreneurial capacity should be undertaken.

The journey through lifelong learning is burdensome for the disabled; the pathways are very rocky and difficult to negotiate. Their aspirations and achievements must be broadened. People with disabilities frequently have difficulty accessing TVE for a range of reasons. These include the underestimation of educators and vocational guidance personnel of the ability and potential of people with disabilities to take up competitive paid employment. Those who are able to join mainstream TVE programmes should be assisted to do so while those with more severe disabilities should be provided with special programmes and learning strategies to realise their potential and optimise their participation in society and the workforce. The commitment to TVE for all requires well designed policies and strategies, increased resources, flexible and appropriate delivery modes, friendly training environments and sensitive and caring teachers and employers.

Roles of Government and Other Stakeholders in TVE

Although governments carry the primary responsibility for TVE, in a modern market economy TVE policy design and delivery must be achieved through a new partnership between government, employers, vocations, industry, trades union and society. This partnership must create a coherent legislative framework to enable the launching of a national strategy for change. Within this strategy the government, apart from actually providing TVE, can fulfil the roles of giving leadership and vision, facilitating, coordinating, establishing quality assurance and ensuring that TVE is for all through identifying and addressing community service obligations. The capacities of the partnerships must be enhanced through training schemes and facilities to impart appropriate skills.

The new partnership should aim to establish a learning culture throughout the society whilst strengthening the economy, achieving social cohesion, helping to maintain cultural identity and diversity and the enhancement of humanity. Training for all occupations directly related to human development should include human rights and responsibilities. The learning culture should enable the establishment and maintenance of an institutional structure which will achieve lifelong learning, wider participation in education and training, and foster the work ethic with a revitalised spirit of entrepreneurship. Both the monetary and non-monetary benefits of TVE should be recognised by government, industry and other stakeholders.

The contribution of the voluntary and NGO sectors to the provision of TVE must be recognised and supported because it constitutes an extremely valuable but often overlooked resource. Government and the private sector must recognise that TVE is an investment, not a cost, with significant returns including the well-being of workers, enhanced productivity and international competitiveness. Therefore, funding for TVE must be shared to the maximum extent possible between government, industry, the community and the learner. There are also opportunities for fund-raising and income-generating activities through collective effort. The mix will vary for each country, but it is important to realise that the benefits of TVE are for all of the partners in society who should therefore take the responsibility to contribute to the creation and ongoing vitality of their TVE system through cost sharing, incorporating appropriate government financial incentives.

A vibrant economy is best served by a diversity of public and private providers of TVE operating in healthy competition, within a national framework of quality assurance. The balance can be struck in many ways but the government should assume responsibility for ensuring strong basic initial vocational preparation no matter which sector is providing its delivery. Government should also be considered a provider of last resort to ensure that potentially excluded populations are not overlooked and are ensured access to TVE programmes. There is a particular need in all countries to expand employment-based training which is well articulated with institutional training through a national framework which includes individual learning credit banks and records, and multiple and flexible entry and exit points.

The private sector has a particularly important role to play in this regard. Within governments there are often shared and overlapping responsibilities for various elements of TVE amongst departments and agencies. It is desirable that governments streamline their own public institutional framework to the maximum extent possible to coordinate the national TVE effort, create an effective partnership with the private sector and promote TVE for the benefit of all stakeholders. All TVE partners will be required to increase constantly their knowledge and expertise in many areas affecting TVE systems.

Effective mechanisms must therefore be established to share experience and expertise through ongoing research of particular relevance for key policy issues. Other approaches may include jointly shared data banks, multimedia technologies, and regional and international cooperation. There is significant scope for countries to share their experience with the design and operation of national TVE policies and strategies, and appropriate public and private roles and partnerships. In this regard there is a need for mutual and co-operative assistance between developing and developed countries and those countries with emerging market economies.

The governments carry the primary responsibility for TVE. In a modern market economy TVE policy design and delivery must be achieved through a new partnership between government, employers, vocations, industry, trades union and society. The role of the state will remain pivotal in creating the necessary enabling environment to enhance the participation of its social partners. This may be achieved through legislation, upgrading policy design and in delivery systems. The state must be concerned principally with the creation of a policy framework for education and training that forms part of the national development plans for change.

A vibrant economy is best served by a diversity of public and private providers of TVE. The combination or balance between the providers may be struck in many ways but the government should ensure strong basic preparation by all providers. Government should also be considered the provider of last resort to ensure that potentially excluded sections of the population are included. Decentralising activities according to the needs of the communities or areas within the country is an important factor in generating new partnerships between employers and the various other sectors of the economy.

This foregoing vision can be effectively reflected by the priorities that governments and their social partners accord the implementation plans and the resources allocated to education and training. The responsibility for the initial basic and vocational preparation shall still remain primarily with the state, and can be designed to ensure employability and retrainability.

In many countries the provision of TVE is the responsibility of several government ministries, and sometimes of different departments even within the same ministry. When the responsibility for TVE is shared in this way coordination mechanisms are required to ensure that the programme is truly national and efficiently conducted with appropriate linkages and articulation between and within different authorities and departments of the government. The role of employers, trade unions and associations in TVE have been changing and growing. Large enterprises and professional associations are active in providing long and short TVE programmes. The quality and effectiveness of such programmes may vary in the industrialised countries, countries in transition, and in those with stable or declining economic growth.

The new vision for TVE should include facilitating the exchange of experiences, data and information on innovative approaches and new roles for employers, unions and professional associations. This could be achieved by creating information networks, and harnessing the multimedia information and communication technologies and data-banks. Employers could enhance their employee retraining programmes to upgrade skills by providing facilities for on-the-job training.

Voluntary organisations and non-governmental organisations (NGOs) make extremely valuable but often overlooked contributions to TVE. The role of NGOs in TVE has been changing dramatically during the last decade. Many NGOs have helped establish formal, non-formal, and informal education and training programmes. NGOs are also increasing their involvement in related areas such as poverty alleviation, employment generation, services for marginalised groups and empowerment of the disabled.

TVE programmes are being used by NGOs as an important avenue for the aforementioned groups to acquire the knowledge and experiences demanded by the world of work. TVE is thus perceived as an effective means of overcoming the social and economic difficulties encountered by these sections of society. The new roles that NGOs are now playing in the field of TVE must be acknowledged and enhanced in order that a new culture of lifelong learning is introduced outside the formal education system. To facilitate better funding of the educational and training sector, the government shall need to develop appropriate tax incentives and other benefits to stimulate and support private sector participation in TVE. Further, the state must ensure that education and training are delivered cost effectively both by itself and its social partners with optimal utilisation of resources.

Financing TVE programmes and projects is an increasingly complex task for governments and other stakeholders. Many member states are facing difficulties in keeping up with the demand for programme expansion, new equipment and the introduction of modern technologies in TVE. However, government and private sector must recognise that TVE is an investment, not a cost. It yields significant returns such as the well-being of workers, enhanced productivity and international competitiveness. Government, industry and other stakeholders must recognise both the monetary and non-monetary benefits of TVE. Funding for TVE must be shared to the maximum extent possible between government, industry, the community and the learner. The human and financial resources allocated for TVE are sometimes diverted, in certain cases, to other parts of the system, which in turn affect TVE quality, effectiveness and efficiency to meet emerging needs. Governments must therefore streamline their institutional framework to achieve a coordinated national TVE system which involves partnership of both private and public partners. All partners in society will benefit from TVE and therefore they should assume the responsibility for the sustained vitality of their TVE system through cost-sharing mechanisms. Widening partnerships between government, its social partners and other stakeholders for the development of TVE for the new millennium is an unavoidable trend. Many sectors of the community must be involved as responsible partners in the development of TVE.

UNESCO'S RECOMMENDATION CONCERNING TECHNICAL AND VOCATIONAL EDUCATION (2001)

I. Scope

1. This Recommendation applies to all forms and aspects of education that are technical and vocational in nature, provided either in educational institutions or under their authority, by public authorities, the private sector or through other forms of organised education, formal or non-formal, aiming to ensure that all members of the community have access to the pathways of lifelong learning.
2. For the purposes of this Recommendation "technical and vocational education" is used as a comprehensive term referring to those aspects of the educational process involving, in addition to general education, the study of technologies and related sciences, and the acquisition of practical skills, attitudes, understanding and knowledge relating to occupations in various sectors of economic and social life. Technical and vocational education is further understood to be:

   a) an integral part of general education;

b) a means of preparing for occupational fields and for effective participation in the world of work;

c) an aspect of lifelong learning and a preparation for responsible citizenship;

d) an instrument for promoting environmentally sound sustainable development;

(e) a method of facilitating poverty alleviation.

3. Technical and vocational education, being part of the total educational process and being a right as described in Article 26 of the Universal Declaration of Human Rights, is included in the term "education" as defined in the Convention Revised Recommendation concerning and the Recommendation against Discrimination in Education adopted by the General Conference of the United Nations Educational, Scientific and Cultural Organisation at its 11th session (1960) and the Convention on Technical and Vocational Education adopted by the General Conference at its 25th session (1989). The provisions of these documents are therefore applicable to it.

4. This Recommendation should be understood as setting forth general principles, goals and guidelines to be applied by each individual country according to its socio-economic needs and available resources in a changing world, with a view also to enhancing the status of technical and vocational education. The application of the provisions and the timing of the implementation will depend upon the specific conditions, and constitutional provisions existing in a given country.

II. Technical and vocational education in relation to the educational process: objectives

5. Given the immense scientific, technological and socio-economic development, either in progress or envisaged, which characterises the present era, particularly globalisation and the revolution in information and

communication technology, technical and vocational education should be a vital aspect of the educational process in all countries, and in particular should:

a) contribute to the achievement of the societal goals of greater democratisation and social, cultural and economic development, while at the same time developing the potential of all individuals, both men and women, for active participation in the establishment and implementation of these goals, regardless of religion, race and age;

b) lead to an understanding of the scientific and technological aspects of contemporary civilisation in such a way that people comprehend their environment and are capable of acting upon it while taking a critical view of the social, political and environmental implications of scientific and technological change;

c) empower people to contribute to environmentally sound sustainable development through their occupations and other areas of their lives.

6. Given the necessity for new relationships between education, the world of work and the community as a whole, technical and vocational education should exist as part of a system of lifelong learning adapted to the needs of each particular country and to worldwide technological development. This system should be directed to:

a) abolishing barriers between levels and areas of education, between education and the world of work, and between school and society through:

i) the appropriate integration of technical/vocational and general education at all levels;

ii) the creation of open and flexible educational structures;

iii) the taking into account of individuals' educational needs, the evolution of occupations and jobs recognising work experience as a part of learning;

(b) improving the quality of life by creating a learning culture that permits individuals to expand their intellectual horizons, to acquire and to constantly improve professional skills and knowledge, and to engage positively in society to utilise the fruits of economic and technological change for the general welfare.

7. Technical and vocational education should begin with a broad base which facilitates horizontal and vertical articulation within the education system and between school and the world of work, thus contributing to the elimination of all forms of discrimination, and should be designed so that it:

a) is an integral part of everyone's basic general education in the form of initiation to technology, the world of work, and human values and standards for responsible citizenship;

b) may be freely and positively chosen as the means by which people develop talents, interests and skills leading to an occupation in various sectors or to further education;

c) allows access to other aspects and areas of education at all levels, including institutions of higher learning, by being grounded in a solid general education and, as a result of the integration containing a general education component through all stages of specialisation;

d) allows transfers from one field to another within technical and vocational education;

e) is readily available to all and for all appropriate types of specialisation, within and outside formal education systems, and in conjunction or in parallel with training in order to permit educational, career and job mobility at the minimum age at which the general basic education is considered to have been acquired, according to the education system in force in each country;.

f) is available on the above terms and on a basis of equality to women as well as men, and where the learning and working environment is made suitable for the participation of girls and women by removing overt and covert bias and discrimination and seeking strategies for motivating girls and women to take an interest in vocational and technical education;

g) is available to people with disabilities and to socially and economically disadvantaged groups such as immigrants, refugees, minorities (including indigenous peoples), demobilised soldiers in post-conflict situations, and underprivileged and marginalised youth in special forms adapted to their needs in order to integrate them more easily into society. In terms of the needs and aspirations of individuals, technical and vocational education should:

   a) permit the harmonious development of personality and character, and foster spiritual and human values, the capacity for understanding, judgement, critical thinking and self-expression;

   b) prepare the individual for lifelong learning by developing the necessary mental tools, technical and entrepreneurial skills and attitudes;

   c) develop capacities for decision making and the qualities necessary for active and intelligent participation, teamwork and leadership at work and in the community as a whole;

   d) enable an individual to cope with the rapid advances in information and communication technology.

III. Policy, planning and administration

9. Policy should be formulated and technical and vocational education administered in support of the general objectives adopted for the educational process as well as

for national and, if possible, the regional social and economic requirements of the present and the future, and an appropriate legislative and financial framework adopted. Policy should be directed to both the structural and the qualitative improvement of technical and vocational education as stipulated in Article 2 of the Convention on Technical and Vocational Education (1989) and further described in the recommendations of the Second International Congress on Technical and Vocational Education (1999):

a) Although governments carry the primary responsibility for technical and vocational education, in a modern market economy technical and vocational education policy design and delivery should be achieved through a new partnership between government, employers, professional associations, industry, employees and their representatives, the local community and non-governmental organisations (NGOs). This partnership must create a coherent legislative framework to enable the launching of a national strategy for change. Within this strategy the government, apart from actually providing technical and vocational education, can also provide leadership and vision, facilitate, coordinate, establish quality assurance and ensure that technical and vocational education is for all by identifying and addressing community service obligations.

b) Technical and vocational education is best served by a diversity of public and private providers. The appropriate mix can be found in many ways, with the responsibility of governments being to facilitate choice while ensuring quality.

c) Government and the private sector should recognise that technical and vocational education is an investment, not a cost, with significant returns, including the well-being of workers, enhanced productivity and international competitiveness.

Therefore funding for technical and vocational education should be shared to the maximum extent possible between government, industry, the community and the learner, with government providing appropriate financial incentives. Furthermore, the governments of least developed countries in particular should seek bilateral and multilateral capacity-building cooperation in technical and vocational education.

d) Within governments, there are often shared and overlapping responsibilities for various elements of technical and vocational education among departments and agencies. It is desirable that governments streamline their own public institutional framework to the maximum extent possible to coordinate the national technical and vocational education effort, create an effective partnership with the private sector, and promote technical and vocational education for the benefit of all stakeholders.

10. Particular attention should be given to planning the development and expansion of technical and vocational education by:

a) giving high priority to technical and vocational education in national development agendas as well as in plans for educational reform;

b) evaluating national short-term and long-term needs;

c) providing appropriate current and future allocations of financial resources;

d) establishing a national body responsible for coordinating planning in technical and vocational education based on analysis of statistical data and projections to facilitate complementarity between educational policy planning and employment policy.

11. Planning should respond to national and, if possible, regional, economic and social trends, to projected changes in demand for different classes of goods and services, and

for different types of skills and knowledge in such a way that technical and vocational education may easily adapt to the evolving scientific, technological and socio-economic changes. This planning should also be coordinated with current and projected training action and the evolution of the world of work in both urban and rural areas.

12. While the education authorities should have primary responsibility, the following groups of relevant stakeholders should be actively associated in policy formulation and in the planning process; corresponding structures, both national and local, taking the form of public agencies or consultative or advisory bodies, should be created to permit this:
    a) public authorities responsible for planning economic and social policy, labour and employment, and for the manufacturing and service sectors;
    b) representatives of non-governmental organisations within each occupation sector from among employers and workers as well as of the informal economy, small enterprise owners and entrepreneurs;
    c) authorities or bodies responsible for out-of-school education and training;
    d) representatives of those responsible—both in public education and in state-recognised private education—for executing educational policy, including teachers, examining bodies and administrators;
    e) parents', former pupils', students' and youth organisations;
    f) representatives from the community at large.

13. Policies for the structural improvement of technical and vocational education should be established within the framework of broad policies designed to implement the principle of lifelong education through the creation of open, flexible and complementary structures for education, training and educational and vocational guidance, considering the provisions of modern information

technology in education regardless of whether these activities take place within the system of formal education or outside it. In this respect, consideration should be given to the following:

a) multi-purpose secondary education offering diversified curricula linking education to the world of work;
b) having institutions of higher learning offering flexible admission and programmes ranging from short specialised ones to longer full-time programmes of integrated studies and professional specialisation;
c) establishing a system of equivalencies whereby credit is given for completion of any approved programme, and recognition is granted to educational and/or professional qualifications and work experience;
d) providing articulation and pathways between technical and vocational education and programmes of higher education for the benefit of those learners who may wish to continue their education.

14. Policy should be directed to ensuring high quality so as to exclude discrimination between the different educational streams. In this respect, special efforts should be made to ensure that national technical and vocational education seeks to meet international standards.

15. In order to ensure quality, responsible national authorities should establish criteria and standards, subject to periodic review and evaluation, applying to all aspects of technical and vocational education, including, to the greatest extent possible, non-formal education for:

a) all forms of recognition of achievement and consequent qualification;
b) staff qualifications;
c) ratios of teaching and training staff to learners;
d) the quality of curricula and teaching materials;
e) safety precautions for all learning and training environments;

f) physical facilities, buildings, libraries, workshop layouts, quality and type of equipment.

16. National policy should foster research related to technical and vocational education, with particular emphasis on its potential within lifelong learning, and directed to its improvement and relevance to the prevailing socio-economic context. This research should be carried out at national and institutional levels, as well as through individual initiative. To this end:

a) special emphasis should be placed on curriculum development, research concerning teaching and learning methods and materials, and, where the need exists, on technologies and techniques applied to development problems;

b) financial resources and physical facilities from public and/or private sources should be made available to institutions of higher education, specialised research institutions and professional organisations for applying the results of this research on an experimental basis in representatively selected institutions for technical and vocational education;

c) the positive results of research and experimentation should be widely disseminated using all available media, especially information and communication technology;

d) the effectiveness of technical and vocational education should be evaluated using, among other data, relevant statistics including those concerning part-time enrolments, dropout rates and placement in wage- and self-employment;

e) research efforts to humanise working conditions should be emphasised.

17. Administrative structures should provide for evaluation, supervisory and accreditation services to ensure the rapid application of new research findings and to maintain standards:

a) evaluation services as a whole should ensure the quality and smooth operation of technical and vocational education by continuous review and action directed to monitoring progress and maintaining standards through constant improvement of staff, facilities, programmes and, most importantly, student achievement;

b) supervisory services for the staff should encourage improvement in the quality of teaching by providing guidance and advice and recommending continuing education;

c) all technical and vocational education programmes, including those offered by private bodies, should be subject to approval by the public authorities;

d) individual institutions should have the autonomy to design their programmes with the involvement of business and industry to suit local needs.

18. Particular attention should be given to the material resources required for technical and vocational education. Priorities should be carefully established with due regard for immediate needs and the probable directions of future expansion in consultation with representatives from the world of work:

a) institutional planning should be directed to ensuring maximum efficiency and flexibility in use;

b) the planning, construction and equipping of facilities should be carried out in collaboration with specialists from industry, teachers and educational architects, and with due regard for the purpose of the facilities, prevailing local factors and relevant research;

c) adequate funds should be allocated for recurrent expenditure for supplies and maintenance and repair of equipment;

d) institutions should be given greater autonomy in their administration and financial management.

IV. Technical and vocational aspects of general education

19. An initiation to technology and to the world of work should be an essential component of general education. An understanding of the technological nature of modern culture and an appreciation of work requiring practical skills should thereby be acquired. This initiation should be a major concern in educational reform and democratisation. It should be a required element in the curriculum, beginning in primary education and continuing through the early years of secondary education.

20. Opportunities for general technical and vocational initiation should continue to be available to those who wish to avail themselves of it within the education system and outside it in places of work or the community at large.

21. Technical and vocational initiation in the general education of youth should fulfil the educational requirements of all spheres of interest and ability. It should mainly perform three functions:

    a) to broaden educational horizons by serving as an introduction to the world of work, and the world of technology and its products through the exploration of materials, tools, techniques, and the process of production, distribution and management as a whole, and to enrich the learning process through practical experience;

    b) to orient those with the interest and ability in technical and vocational education towards preparation for an occupational field or training outside the formal education system;

    c) to promote in those who will leave formal education with no specific occupational aims or skills, attitudes and thought processes likely to enhance their aptitudes and potential, to facilitate the choice of an occupation and access to a first job, and to permit them to continue their vocational training and personal development.

22. General technical and vocational studies in schools, having great importance for the orientation and education of youth programmes, should include an appropriate balance between theoretical and practical work. Such a programme of studies should be drawn up in collaboration with the professional community and with those responsible for technical and vocational education. These programmes should:
    a) be based upon a problem-solving and experimental approach, and involve experience in planning methods and decision making;
    b) introduce the learner to a broad spectrum of technological fields and to productive work situations;
    c) develop a certain command of valuable practical skills such as tool use, repair and maintenance and safety procedures, and a respect for their value;
    d) develop an appreciation of good design, craftsmanship and quality;
    e) develop the ability to function as a team member and to communicate technical information;
    f) be closely related to the local environment without, however, being limited to it.

23. Technical and vocational initiation programmes in general educational enrichment for youth and adults should be directed to enabling those engaged in working life to:
    a) understand the general implications of technical change, its impact on their professional and private lives, and how to adapt to these changes;
    b) use practical skills for improving the home and community environment, and thus the quality of life and productive leisure-time activities;
    c) inculcate an awareness of the possible impact of technology on the environment, and of the concept of sustainable development.

V. Technical and vocational education as preparation for an occupational field

24. Given the disparities that may exist between formal education, whether secondary or tertiary, and the employment and career opportunities available, the highest priority should be given to technical and vocational education. Consequently the structure and content of traditional education, whether general or technical and vocational, should be adapted accordingly through:
    a) the diversification of secondary education in the later stages so that it may be pursued in conjunction with employment or training, or may lead to employment or to higher education, thereby offering to all youth educational options corresponding to their needs and abilities;
    b) the development of educational structures and programmes on all levels centred on organised and flexible interchange between educational institutions (including universities), training institutions and the world of work.
25. Technical and vocational education as preparation for an occupational field should provide the foundation for productive and satisfying careers and should:
    a) lead to the acquisition of broad knowledge and generic skills applicable to a number of occupations within a given field so that the individual is not limited in his choice of occupation and is able to transfer from one field to another during his/her working life;
    b) at the same time offer both a thorough and specialised preparation for initial employment, including self-employment, and also training within employment;
    c) provide the background in terms of knowledge, skills and attitudes for continuing education at any point in the individual's working life.

26. Premature and narrow specialisation should be avoided:
    a) in principle, the age of 15 should be considered the lower limit for beginning specialisation;
    b) a period of common studies providing basic knowledge and generic skills should be required for each broad occupational sector before a special branch is chosen.

27. Technical and vocational education programmes should be designed as comprehensive and inclusive systems to accommodate the needs of all learners with special emphasis on motivating girls and women. Their equal access and participation should be ensured by:
    a) appropriate legislative measures;
    b) widespread dissemination of information concerning opportunities;
    c) gender-sensitive guidance and counselling;
    d) other incentives relevant to the local context.

28. Special provision should be made for out-of-school and unemployed youth and children of socially disadvantaged groups such as minorities, migrant workers, refugees, etc., with little or no primary education, as well as for those not entering education or training programmes after completion of compulsory schooling, in order that they may acquire skills for wage- or self-employment.

29. Given the necessity of integrating people who are disadvantaged due to physical and intellectual disabilities into society and its occupations, the same educational opportunities should be available to them as to those without disabilities in order that they may achieve qualification for an occupation to realise their potential and optimise their participation in the work force; special measures or special institutions may be required.

Organisation

30. Technical and vocational education as preparation for an occupational field should be organised on a national or

provincial/local basis, so as to respond positively to overall social, economic and educational requirements and to the needs of different groups of the population without discrimination.

31. Several organisational patterns of technical and vocational education, including full-time, part-time, open and distance learning options, could exist within each country. The following patterns should be considered:

   a) full-time programmes including general education and practical training, provided in an educational establishment, either comprehensive or specialised;

   b) part-time programmes such as the following, in which general education and theoretical and broad practical aspects of the occupational field are given in an educational establishment, while specialised practical training is acquired during work in the chosen occupation:

      i) the day-release system, providing for workers and apprentices to attend an educational establishment one or two days a week;

      ii) the sandwich system, under which periods in an educational institution alternate with training periods in a factory, farm, business establishment or other undertaking;

      iii) the block-release system, whereby workers are released to attend courses of 10 to 15 weeks per year.

   c) open and distance education programmes provided through:

      i) correspondence;

      ii) special radio and television broadcasting;

      iii) the Internet and other computer-based media.

32. The responsible authorities should encourage part-time education; therefore:

a) these programmes could be available after completion of minimum compulsory or required schooling, and should continue to be available throughout life;

b) the qualifications acquired by this means should be equivalent to those acquired by full-time education;

c) the practical training conducted by employers should be as broad as possible, and should aim to meet international standards.

33. In view of the increasing requirement for qualified middle-level personnel and the increasing numbers completing secondary education or its equivalent, the development of technical and vocational programmes at a tertiary level should be given high priority, by both public and private providers. The following patterns should be considered:

a) a period of one to two years of guided work experience followed by part-time or full-time programmes of specialisation;

b) part-time and/or evening programmes;

c) full-time programmes as an extension to those given in specialised secondary or tertiary institutions; and

d) programmes offered through open and distance learning.

34. In view of the high cost of equipment, its usage should be organised to yield optimum benefit. This could be achieved as follows:

a) centralised or mobile workshops and libraries could be used to serve several educational institutions;

b) when educational institutions close for the evenings and vacations, their classrooms and workshops should be utilised for continuing education and non-formal training programmes;

c) workshops and laboratories should also be used to instil the culture of maintenance and respect for safety standards;

d) enterprises should be encouraged to make their equipment and facilities available for practical training.

35. Enterprises should be actively involved in the theoretical and practical training of those preparing for occupations in their particular sector, and should interact with educational institutions regarding the organisation of such training.

Programme content

36. All programmes of technical and vocational education as preparation for an occupational field should:

a) aim at providing scientific knowledge, technical versatility and a cluster of core competencies and generic skills required for rapid adaptation to new ideas and procedures and for steady career development;

b) be based on analyses and forecasts of occupational requirements by national education authorities, employment authorities, occupational organisations and other stakeholders;

c) include an appropriate balance between general subjects, science and technology, as well as subjects such as computer literacy, information and communication technology, the environment and studies of both the theoretical and practical aspects of the occupational field;

d) stress developing a sense of values, ethics and attitudes to prepare the learner for self-reliance and responsible citizenship.

37. In particular, programmes should:

a) be interdisciplinary in character, as many occupations now require two or more traditional areas of study;

b) be based on curricula designed around core knowledge, competencies and skills;

c) include studies of the social and economic aspects of the occupational field as a whole;

d) include an interdisciplinary perspective to equip students to work in the changing employment environment, and incorporate a multicultural perspective, which may include the study of a foreign language as preparation for international employment;

e) include the study of at least one foreign language of international use, which, while conducive to a higher cultural level, will give special emphasis to the requirements of communication, the acquisition of a scientific and technical vocabulary, and the need to prepare for international employment and multicultural working environments;

f) include an introduction to organisational, planning and entrepreneurial skills;

g) emphasise instruction in safe and environmentally sound procedures relative to the materials and equipment used in a given occupational field, the importance of safe working conditions, and the health aspects relative to the occupation as a whole, including emergency and first-aid training.

38. While based on the above general principles and components, and thus pursuing in all cases broader educational aims, programmes in their practical aspect should be designed taking into account special occupational requirements, especially in "new" professions and those undergoing change, and particularly the use of the new information and communication technology as a tool for enhancing the effectiveness of all vocations, including those considered traditional.

39. Technical and vocational education programmes leading to university qualification, while encouraging research and offering high-level specialisation, should be developed with particular attention to:

a) the inclusion of components directed to developing attitudes whereby those with broad responsibilities in technological fields constantly relate their professional tasks to broader social and ethical goals;

b) preparing the learner more generally for life and the world of work bearing in mind that technical and vocational education is for economic, personal and social benefit.

40. Programmes of technical and vocational education as preparation for occupations within the agricultural sector should be designed in accordance with the overall social and economic requirements of sustainable development in rural areas.

41. Where lack of resources is a serious constraint, priority should be given to developing programmes for areas experiencing skilled human resource shortages, taking into consideration the projected needs for national economic development and the corresponding labour market growth.

42. Programmes preparing for occupations in small industry, individual farming or the artisan trades, particularly for self-employment, should include entrepreneurship and elementary information and communication technology studies to enable those engaged in such occupations to take responsibility for production, marketing, competent management and the rational organisation of the enterprise.

43. Programmes leading to occupations in the business, commercial and service sector, including the tourism and hospitality industries, should consist of:

a) training in the methods and skills developed as a result of the application of computer-based technology to business and office management, and particularly to the acquisition and processing of information;

b) training in the organisational and management skills required for the smooth operation of enterprises;

c) an introduction to marketing and distribution procedures.

44. Special attention should be given to developing programmes for preparing personnel at all levels for the social services system (e.g., community and family work, nursing and paramedical occupations, nutrition and food technology, home economics and environmental improvement). Those programmes should:

a) orientate the special occupational field to raising standards of living in terms of nutrition, clothing, housing, medical services, the quality of family life and that of the environment;

b) be adapted to the special requirements of local conditions, in particular those of climate and geography, materials available, community organisation, and social and cultural patterns.

VI. Technical and vocational education as continuing education

45. The development and expansion of technical and vocational education as continuing education, both within and outside the formal education system, with either public or private funding, and within the framework of lifelong learning, should be a priority objective of all educational strategies. Broad provision should be made for allowing everyone, whatever their prior qualifications, to continue both their professional and general education by facilitating seamless pathways for learners through articulation, accreditation and recognition of all prior learning and relevant work experience. Technical and vocational education should develop close interfaces with all other educational sectors. Within this spectrum, technical and vocational education has a responsibility to ensure a sound initial education and training aimed at learning to learn, the most precious skill for all citizens,

both young and adult. In addition to permitting adults to make up deficiencies in general or vocational education, which has often been its sole objective, continuing education should now:

a) offer possibilities for personal development and professional advancement by providing flexibility in programme administration and curriculum design to facilitate smooth lifelong learning and ensure continuous entry, exit and re-entry points;

b) permit the updating and renewal of knowledge and practical abilities and skills in the occupational field;

c) enable individuals to adapt to technological changes in their occupation or to enter another occupation;

d) be available throughout the individuals' working life without restriction with regard to age, sex, prior education and training or position, recognising work experience as a substitute for prior learning;

e) be available to the increasing numbers of the aged population;

f) be broad in scope, including general education elements and contemporary cross-cutting areas.

47. The appropriate authorities should be encouraged to provide the basic conditions for continuing technical and vocational education, such as providing for paid educational leave and other forms of financial aid.

48. Continuing technical and vocational education should be actively encouraged through:

a) widespread dissemination of information concerning the programmes available and ways of taking advantage of existing opportunities, including full use of the mass media and the internet;

b) recognition of successful completion of programmes by increased remuneration and professional advancement, with the involvement of employers and professional associations.

49. Organisers of continuing technical and vocational education should consider the following flexible forms of delivery:

a) courses and training offered during working hours at the workable;
b) part-time courses utilising existing secondary and tertiary technical and vocational education institutions;
c) evening and weekend courses;
d) correspondence courses;
e) courses on educational radio and television and the internet; and
f) short professional "refresher" courses.

50. The following forms of study/training leave from work should be considered:

a) day release;
b) block release of varying lengths;
c) release for one or more hours during the working day.

51. Programmes of continuing technical and vocational education should:

a) be designed and delivered to suit the special requirements of adults using flexible teaching methods that recognise already acquired expertise;
b) be designed for individually paced learning;
c) be programmed to accommodate the potential that information and communication technology has to offer.

52. Provision should be made for the particular requirements of special groups:

a) to enable women completing maternity leave to update their knowledge and professional skills for re-entering the workhorse;
b) to enable older workers and the unemployed to adapt to new occupations;

c) to provide minorities, foreign workers, migrants, refugees, indigenous people and people with disabilities with training programmes to help them to adapt to working life;

d) to enable other marginalised and excluded groups, such as early school leaves, out-of-school youth and demobilised soldiers in post-conflict situations to re-enter the mainstream of society.

53. Continuing technical and vocational education programmes through the distance learning mode should be promoted for the benefit of those disadvantaged by distance and location, such as individuals in rural communities and those engaged in seasonal work.

VII. Guidance

54. Guidance should be viewed as a continuous process spanning the entire education system, and should be directed towards aiding all to make conscious and positive educational and occupational choices. It should ensure that individuals are provided with the prerequisites:

a) to become aware of their interests, abilities and special talents, and to help them frame a plan for life;

b) to pursue courses of education and training designed to realise their potential and fulfil their life plans;

c) to acquire flexibility in decision making concerning their occupations, in the initial and later stages, for developing a satisfying career;

d) to facilitate transitions back and forth as needed, between education, training and the world of work.

55. Guidance should take into account the needs of industry, the individual and the family while preparing students and adults for the real possibility of frequent career changes, which could include periods of unemployment and employment in the informal sector, to be achieved through:

a) close liaison and coordination between lifelong learning, training, wordplay and placement services;

b) ensuring that all necessary information concerning the world of work and career opportunities is available, and actively disseminated using all available forms of communication;

c) ensuring that those engaged in work have access to information concerning continuing education and training as well as other work opportunities.

56. While emphasising the needs of individuals, guidance should be accompanied by information that gives them a realistic view of the opportunities available, including trends in the labour market and employment structures, the environmental impact of various occupations, and what may be expected in terms of remuneration, career advancement and occupational mobility.

57. Particular attention should be given to guidance for girls and women to ensure that:

a) guidance is gender-inclusive and covers the whole range of education, training and employment opportunities;

b) girls and women are encouraged and motivated to take advantage of the opportunities available;

c) girls and women are encouraged to pursue subjects such as mathematics and science, which are prerequisites for vocational education and training programmes.

58. Guidance in the formal schooling context should promote technical and vocational education as a viable and attractive choice for young people. It should:

a) cover a broad range of occupations, include supplementary visits to workaholics, and make the students aware of the eventual necessity of choosing an occupation and the importance of ensuring that this choice is made as rationally as possible;

b) assist students and their parents/guardians in making a positive choice concerning educational streams, and encourage learners to keep open a wide range of options so as to increase their learning and occupational flexibility.

59. Guidance in technical and vocational education as preparation for an occupational field should:
   a) inform students of the various possibilities open in the particular field of interest, the educational background required, and the subsequent possibilities for continuing education and further training;
   b) encourage students to choose educational programmes that will not limit their later employment options;
   c) follow the students' progress through their educational programmes;
   d) supplement the programmes by short periods of work experience and study of real work situations.

60. For individuals engaged in continuing technical and vocational education as a part of their lifelong learning, guidance should:
   a) help them to choose the programme best suited to their needs;
   b) enable them to make effective choices regarding their entry into suitable levels of specialisation.

61. Guidance should take into account:
   a) economic, social, technological, cultural and family factors influencing the learners' attitudes, expectations and choice of career;
   b) results of testing, including aptitude tests;
   c) educational achievements and/or work experience;
   d) opportunities and prospects in the occupational sector of interest;
   e) individual preferences and special needs, including medical conditions, physical limitations and disabilities.

62. Guidance systems need to be accountable to the beneficiaries and sponsors of the service. Quality assurance and long-term results should be continually monitored at national and institutional levels through:

a) accurate records of clients, needs addressed, programmes and interventions used and resultant employment including self-employment;

b) a system of evaluation both of staff performance and of the methods used to determine the long-term effects of guidance and the degree of self-reliance of beneficiaries.

VIII. Learning process

63. The challenges facing technical and vocational education in the twenty-first century demand learner-centred innovative and flexible approaches including a rearranged curriculum to take account of new subjects and issues such as technology, environment, foreign languages and cultures, entrepreneurship and requirements of rapidly growing service industries.

64. Theory and practice should form an integrated whole and be presented in a manner that motivates the learners. Experience in the laboratory, workshop and/or enterprises should be linked to mathematical and scientific foundations, and conversely, technical theory, as well as the mathematics and science underlying it, should be illustrated through their practical applications.

65. Full use should be made of contemporary educational technology, particularly the internet, interactive multimedia materials, audiovisual aids and mass media, to enhance the reach, cost-effectiveness, quality and richness of programmes, especially in the promotion of self-learning.

66. The methods and materials used in technical and vocational education should be carefully adapted to the learners' needs. In this respect:

a) where the language of instruction differs from the native language, teaching materials should make maximum use of numerical and graphical representation, written material being kept to a minimum;

b) where materials developed in one country are adapted for use in another, this adaptation should be carefully made with due regard to local factors;

c) considering, however, the increasing mobility of labour, the acquisition of foreign language skills should be considered a vital aspect of the curriculum.

67. Machines and equipment used in workshops in educational institutions should be geared to the needs of the workable, and should simulate it as closely as possible. Learners should be capable of operating and maintaining the equipment.

68. Evaluation/assessment should be an integral part of the teaching and learning process, and its major function should be to ensure the availability of appropriate programmes for the development of learners in accordance with their interests and capacities, and competence in the world of work.

69. The learners' performance should be evaluated/assessed on an overall basis that considers class participation, interests and attitude, aptitude for acquiring practical skills and competencies, and relative progress, allowance being made for aptitudes and examinations and other tests.

70. Learners should participate in the evaluation/assessment of their own progress, and this system should have an in-built feedback mechanism to identify and correct learning problems.

71. Continuous evaluation of the teaching and learning process, including formative assessment, should be undertaken with the participation of teachers, supervisors, learners and representatives from the occupational fields

concerned to ensure that the programme is effective and that the knowledge and skills imparted meet the needs of the workplace, and include recent developments in the field of study.

IX. Staff

72. To ensure the high quality of technical and vocational education, priority should be given to the recruitment and initial preparation of adequate numbers of well-qualified teachers, instructors/trainers, administrators and guidance staff, and to the provision of continuous professional upgrading throughout their career, and other facilities to enable them to function effectively.

73. The emoluments and conditions of service which are offered should compare favourably with those enjoyed by persons with similar qualifications and experience in other occupational sectors. In particular, promotions, salaries and pension scales for technical and vocational education staff should take into account any relevant experience acquired in employment outside the educational sector.

Teaching staff

74. All teachers in technical and vocational education, including instructors/trainers who teach practical skills, should be considered an integral part of the teaching profession, and should be recognised as having the same status as their colleagues in general education. In this regard:

   a) the Recommendation concerning the Status of Teachers adopted by the Special Intergovernmental Conference on the Status of Teachers on 5 October 1966 is applicable to them especially as regards the provisions concerning preparation for a profession, continuing education, employment and career, the rights and responsibilities of teachers, conditions for effective teaching and learning, teachers' salaries, and social security;

b) arbitrary distinctions between teachers in specialised technical and vocational institutions and those in general education institutions should be eliminated.

75. Technical and vocational education teachers, on a full-time or part-time basis, should possess the appropriate personal, ethical, professional and teaching qualities, and a strong initial preparation that will enable them to operate in and adapt to an ever-changing scientific, technological and social environment.

76. Teachers of technical and vocational subjects in general education should:

a) be familiar with a broad range of specialities;

b) develop the ability to relate these to each other as well as to the larger social, economic, environmental, historical and cultural context;

c) where these subjects serve primarily an occupation or educational orientation function, be able to give guidance.

77. Teachers of technical and vocational education for occupational fields should have relevant qualifications so that:

a) if the occupational field requires primarily practical skills, they should have significant experience in the exercise of these skills;

b) if learners are to be prepared for technician or middle-management positions, teachers should have a thorough knowledge, preferably acquired through appropriate practical experience, of the special requirements of this type of position;

c) if the occupational field requires research and theoretical analysis, e.g., an engineering field, teachers should have a background in research methods.

78. Teachers in technical and vocational education as continuing education should, in addition to the special

preparation for teaching adults, have an adequate knowledge of the working environment of the learners, and be able to provide distance and individually paced education and training.

79. Skilled professionals working outside education should be invited to teach in schools, universities or other educational institutions in order to link the world of work more closely to the classroom.

80. Teachers of general subjects in technical and vocational education institutions, in addition to qualifications in their own field, should have an appreciation of the nature of the learners' specialised technical and vocational education programme.

81. Preparation for technical and vocational teaching should preferably be offered as a tertiary programme, requiring completion of secondary education or its equivalent for entrance. All programmes should be designed with the following objectives in mind:

    a) to maintain standards of education and professional preparation in effect for the teaching profession as a whole and to contribute to raising these overall standards;

    b) to develop in future teachers the ability to teach both the theoretical and the practical aspects of their field, with special emphasis on the need to use, whenever possible, the information and communication technologies;

    c) to develop in future teachers the responsibility for keeping uptodate with trends in their field, as well as with the related work opportunities;

    d) to develop in future teachers the ability to guide learners with special needs;

    e) to ensure that future teachers are equipped, by means of supplementary training, to teach other subjects related to their primary subject.

82. Flexible training and retraining programmes, combining instruction on the campus and in the workplace, must be adapted to suit the concerned subjects and the needs of the learners and the workplace by developing new and appropriate instruments of assessment, accreditation and articulation, and certification standards.

83. When local conditions prevent future teachers from receiving practical work experience in their training, the teacher-training institution should attempt to simulate workplace conditions as part of the curriculum.

84. The professional preparation of all technical and vocational teachers should include the following elements in pre-service training and in-service upgrading programmes:

   a) educational theory in general and particularly as it applies to technical and vocational education;

   b) educational psychology and sociology relevant to the subjects/fields to be taught by the future teachers;

   c) classroom management, special teaching methods appropriate to the subjects/fields of the future teachers and methods of evaluating/ assessing the students' work;

   d) training in the choice and use of contemporary teaching technique and aids, including information/ communication technologies;

   e) training in how to create and produce appropriate teaching materials, including modular and computer-aided instructional materials, whenever such materials are in short supply;

   f) a period of supervised practice teaching before appointment to a post;

   g) an introduction to educational and occupational guidance methods as well as to educational administration;.

h) planning the instructional environment of practical classes and laboratories and managing/maintaining these facilities;

i) a sound training in safety, with emphasis on teaching safe working practice and setting a good working example.

85. Staff responsible for the preparation of technical and vocational teachers should have obtained advanced qualifications in their field:

a) teacher-educators responsible for special technical and vocational fields should have qualifications in their field equivalent to those of special subjects staff in other higher education institutions and programmes, including advanced degrees and employment experience in related occupational fields;

b) teacher-educators responsible for the pedagogical aspect of teacher preparation should themselves be experienced teachers in technical and vocational education, and should possess advanced qualifications in education.

86. Staff responsible for the preparation of technical and vocational teachers should be actively engaged in technical research and analyses of work opportunities in their field. Provision should be made for this in terms of a reasonable teaching load, and access to appropriate facilities.

87. Teaching staff should be encouraged to continue their education and training, whatever their specialised field, and should have the necessary means to do so. Lifelong learning should be made available in a wide range of facilities, and should include:

a) continuous review and updating of knowledge, competencies and skills;

b) continuous updating of specialised professional skills and knowledge;

c) periodic work experience in the relevant occupational sector.

88. When questions of promotion, seniority and status are considered, teachers' achievements in continuing education and training as well as relevant work experience should be taken into account.

Administrative and guidance staff

89. Administrators of technical and vocational education programmes should be equipped with the following qualifications:

    a) teaching experience in a field of technical and vocational education;

    b) some work experience in one of the fields taught in the programme;

    c) a broad vision of technical and vocational education as a vital element in personal, social and economic development;

    d) knowledge of administrative techniques and procedures.

90. The heads of technical and vocational education establishments should devote a significant portion of their time to the educational and scientific aspects of their work. Sufficient staff should be available to provide the following services:

    a) counselling and guidance for candidates and students;

    b) the preparation, supervision and coordination of all practical work and experiments;

    c) the maintenance of instruments, apparatus and tools in workshops and laboratories;

    d) academic support services such as libraries, information and communication technology centres and information resource centres.

91. Administrators should keep up to date with new administrative techniques and trends, especially through relevant lifelong learning programmes. They should

receive special training in the methods and problems associated with the specific features of technical and vocational education programmes, such as flexible entry and re-entry patterns, continuous training in the workplace, and relevance to the needs of the world of work. This preparation should include:

a) management methods appropriate to educational administration, including techniques that utilise information and communication technologies;

b) financial planning methods that facilitate the allocation of available resources, given the objectives and priorities of the various programmes, and ensure their efficient utilisation;

c) contemporary human resources management and development methods.

92. Guidance staff should receive special preparation for their tasks. They should be equipped to make objective assessments of aptitude, interest and motivation, and have uptodate information concerning education and work opportunities. They should acquire a direct knowledge of the economy and the world of work through systematically organised visits to enterprises and training periods in enterprises. Guidance staff should be provided with facilities—including the opportunity for practical experience—to keep up with new information and methods of guidance. Most importantly, they should bear in mind the concept that technical and vocational education must be available to all as part of the lifelong learning process. It must contribute to personal and economic development and responsible citizenship.

X. International cooperation

93. Member states should give priority to international cooperation between the North and the South, as well as between countries of the South, with the assistance of concerned international organisations, to renovate and

sustain technical and vocational education systems, with particular emphasis on the following:

a) the need for developing countries to take ownership of technical and vocational education and to increase their budget for this sector of education;

b) the efficient coordination, within any given country, of international assistance activities;

c) enhancing the sharing of intellectual property, including through research and development, for the benefit of learners in all countries and situations;

d) recognition by all stakeholders, including international financial authorities, of the contribution of technical and vocational education to the maintenance of peace and stability and to the prevention of social dysfunction, and the need to incorporate support for this sector of education in their assistance to recipient countries.

94. Member states should take special measures to make technical and vocations education accessible to foreigners (in particular migrants and refugees) and their children living within their territory. Such measures should take into account the special needs of such persons in the host country, as well as in the event of their return to their country of origin.

95. There is significant scope for countries to share their experience in technical and vocational education. There is a need for mutual cooperative assistance between all countries, regardless of their state of development. Provision should be made at the national, regional and international levels for the regular exchange, making use of contemporary information and communication technologies, of information, documentation, and materials obtained from research and development, in particular:

a) publications concerning comparative education, psychological and pedagogical problems affecting general and technical and vocational education, and current trends;

b) information and documentation concerning curriculum development, methods and materials, study opportunities abroad, and employment opportunities, including human resource requirements, working conditions and social benefits;

c) ideas, innovations and new teaching/learning/training materials;

d) mass media programmes of an informational or pedagogical character.

96. Regional cooperation should be encouraged among countries having a common cultural heritage and/or facing common problems in the development or extension of technical and vocational education through:

a) periodic meetings at the ministerial level, and the establishment of a mechanism to review policies formulated and actions taken;

b) the creation of joint facilities for higher level research, the development of prototype materials and equipment, and the preparation of staff for the training of teachers where the costs of such facilities are too high to be sustained by any one country.

97. The development of teaching and learning materials which use the information and communication technologies and are suitable for international or regional use should be considered a priority area. These materials should contribute to the progressive establishment and recognition of common standards for professional competencies/qualifications acquired through technical and vocational education. Moreover, such teaching and learning materials should encourage deliberate international collaborative teaching and learning among institutions.

98. Member states should encourage the creation of a climate favourable to international cooperation with a view to

capacity-building in developing countries, especially in the areas of acquisition, adaptation and application of technology, through:

a) fellowship and exchange programmes for teachers/trainers, students and administrators/managers;
b) establishing sustained cooperation between similar institutions in different countries, such as through twinning arrangements;
c) provision of work experience abroad, particularly when opportunities at home are limited;
d) encouraging countries to present and make known their educational programmes outside their national boundaries.

99. To facilitate international cooperation, member states should, through the exchange of good practices and methods, aim to apply relevant and appropriate internationally recommended standards and norms relating in particular to:

a) systems of assessment/evaluation;
b) scientific and technical symbols;
c) occupational qualifications and certification;
d) equipment and technical standards;
e) information processing;
f) equivalencies of qualifications implying standardisation of curricula and testing, including aptitude tests;
g) occupational safety and security through testing of materials, products and processes;
h) environmental protection and conservation.

100. Internationally recommended standards and norms should be continuously evaluated through sustained research on and monitoring of the effectiveness of their application in each country, with a view to enabling countries to use lifelong technical and vocational education

as a means of narrowing the disparities between the North and the South and as a bridge to a more prosperous and peaceful future in the twenty-first century.

Training and Development

1. A critical challenge that faces human society at the start of the twenty-first century is to attain full employment and sustained economic growth in the global economy and social arena. The ILO's framework of decent work addresses both the quality and quantity of employment and provides a basis for new education and training policies and strategies. Human resources development, education and training contribute significantly to promoting the interests of individuals, enterprises, economy and society. By making individuals employable and informed citizens, human resources development and training contribute to economic development and to achieving full employment and promoting social inclusion. They also help individuals to gain access to decent work and good jobs, and escape poverty and marginalisation. Education and skills formation could lead to less unemployment and to more equity in employment. The economy and society at large, like individuals and enterprises, benefit from human resources development and training. The economy becomes more productive, innovative and competitive through the existence of more skilled human potential. Human resources development and training also underpin the fundamental values of society—equity, justice, gender equality, non-discrimination, social responsibility, and participation.
2. Technological changes, changes in financial markets, the emergence of global markets for products and services, international competition, dramatic increases in foreign direct investment, new business strategies, new management practices, new forms of business organisation and of the organisation of work are among the more significant developments that are transforming the world

of work. Many of these developments are also components of globalisation which is the name given to the various processes producing the dramatically increased integration of economic activity in the world today. These developments offer both opportunities and challenges for enterprises, workers and countries. For enterprises increased competition has meant more winners and losers. For countries globalisation has increased both national development and disadvantages as globalisation has exacerbated differences in the relative advantages of countries. For some workers these developments have resulted in career opportunities or successful self-employment, improved living standards and prosperity but for other workers they have resulted in job insecurity or unemployment, declining living standards and poverty. Many of these developments are dramatically increasing the importance of the application of human knowledge and skills to economic activity. Human resources development, education and training are necessary and essential elements required to take both full advantage of the opportunities and to rise to the challenges of these developments for enterprises, workers and countries. There is a growing recognition that globalisation has a social dimension that requires a social response. Education and training are components to both the economic and social response to globalisation.

3. Education and training cannot alone address this challenge, but should go hand-in-hand with economic, employment and other policies to establish, in an equitable manner, the new knowledge and skills-based society in the global economy. Education and training have distinct but converging outcomes as society is changing. They have both a dual rationale: develop skills and knowledge that will help countries, enterprises and individuals utilise the new opportunities and enhance the employability, productivity and income-earning capacity of many population groups that have been adversely affected by

globalisation and changes in society at large. Education and training are necessary for economic and employment growth and social development. They also contribute to personal growth and provide the foundation of an informed citizenry. Education and training are a means to empower people, improve the quality and organisation of work, enhance citizens' productivity, raise workers' incomes, improve enterprise competitiveness, promote job security and social equity. Education and training are therefore a central pillar of decent work. Education and training help individuals become more employable in rapidly changing internal and external labour markets.

4. Human resources training and development are fundamental, but are by themselves insufficient to ensure sustainable economic and social development, or resolve the aggregate employment challenge. They should be coherent and form an integrated part of comprehensive economic labour market and social policies and programmes that promote economic and employment growth. Policies that expand aggregate demand in the economy such as macrocosmic and other measures must be combined with supply-side policies, e.g., science and technology, education and training, and industrial and enterprise policies. Appropriate fiscal policies, social security and collective bargaining are among the means to distribute these economic gains on a fair and equitable basis, and constitute basic incentives to invest in training. Pursuing these integrated policies requires consideration of a new financial and social architecture for the global economy, a subject for ILO research.

5. It is the task of basic education to ensure to each individual the full development of the human personality and citizenship; and to lay the foundation for employability. Initial training develops further his employability by providing general core work skills, and the underpinning knowledge, and industry-based and professional competencies which are portable and

facilitate the transition into the world of work. Lifelong learning ensures that the individual's skills and competencies are maintained and improved as work, technology and skill requirements change; ensures the personal and career development of workers; results in increases in aggregate productivity and income; and improves social equity. Both in developed countries as well as in developing countries there are many workers without the basic skills for literacy and numeracy. National and international strategies have to be developed to eliminate illiteracy, based on concrete targets, benchmarks and quality assessment.

6. Education and training of high quality are major instruments to improve overall socio-economic conditions and to prevent and combat social exclusion and discrimination, particularly in employment. In order to be effective they must cover everyone, including disadvantaged groups. Therefore, they must be carefully targeted at women and persons with special needs, including rural workers; people with disabilities; older workers; the long-term unemployed, including low-skilled workers; young people; migrant workers; and workers laid off as a result of economic reform programmes, or industrial and enterprise restructuring. In addressing the needs of these groups, particularly of young people, access to a combination of formal, off-the-job, and workplace learning should be systematically offered and developed as it provides for effective learning outcomes and increases the chance of entering the labour market.

7. Training can be one of the instruments that, together with other measures, address the challenge of the informal sector. The informal sector is not a sector in the traditional sense of economic classification but a name given to the economic activity of persons in a variety of situations, most of which are survival activities. Informal sector work is unprotected work that is, for the most part, characterised by low earnings and low productivity. The role of training

is not to prepare people for the informal sector and keep them there; or to expand the informal sector; but rather it should go in conjunction with other instruments, such as fiscal policies, provision of credit, and extension of social protection and labour laws, to improve the performance of enterprises and the employability of workers in order to transform what are often marginal, survival activities into decent work fully integrated into mainstream economic life. Prior learning and skills gained in the sector should be validated, as they will help the said workers gain access to the formal labour market. The social partners should be fully involved in developing these programmes.

8. Education and training are a right for all. Governments, in cooperation with the social partners, should ensure that this right is universally accessible. It is the responsibility of all persons to make use of the opportunities offered. Free universal, quality public primary and secondary education must be made available to all children, and they should not be denied sustained access to education through child labour. Education cannot be separated from training. Basic and secondary education is the foundation on which an effective vocational education and training system should be built. Good quality basic education and initial training, availability of adult and second chance education, together with a learning culture, ensure high levels of participation in continuous education and training. Qualified teachers and trainers are the fundamental key to providing quality education for helping children and adults reach high standards in academic and vocational competencies. Their recruitment, remuneration, education, training and retraining, assignment and provision of adequate facilities are critical elements of any successful educational system. In addition to education and training, career guidance and job placement services (career development services) embracing career education, career counselling,

employment counselling and educational, vocational and labour market information, all have a crucial role to play in human resources development. The fostering of a career development culture throughout education, training systems as well as employment services is a means to promote continuous learning. The development of this culture among youth and adults will be of particular importance for ensuring their employability and facilitating their transition from education and training to work or further training.

9. Employability is defined broadly. It is a key outcome of education and training of high quality, as well as a range of other policies. It encompasses the skills, knowledge and competencies that enhance a worker's ability to secure and retain a job, progress at work and cope with change, secure another job if he so wishes or has been laid off, and enter more easily into the labour market at different periods of the lifecycle. Individuals are most employable when they have broad-based education and training, basic and portable high-level skills, including teamwork, problem solving, information and communications technology (ICT) and communication and language skills, learning to learn skills, and competencies to protect themselves and their colleagues against occupational hazards and diseases. This combination of skills enables them to adapt to changes in the world of work. Employability also covers multiple skills that are essential to secure and retain decent work. Entrepreneurship can contribute to creating opportunities for employment and hence to employability. Employability is, however, not a function only of training—it requires a range of other instruments which results in the existence of jobs, the enhancement of quality jobs, and sustainable employment. Workers' employability can only be sustained in an economic environment that promotes job growth and rewards individual and collective investments in human resources training and development.

10. There is tripartite and international consensus about guaranteeing universal access of all to, and increasing and optimising overall investment in, basic education, initial training and continuous training. Discrimination which limits access to training should be combated both by anti-discrimination regulations as well as by common action of social partners. These principles have been endorsed already in the Tripartite Declaration of Principles concerning Multinational Enterprises and Social Policy adopted by the Governing Body, 1977. The Committee endorsed the core commitments made in the Cologne Charter of the Group of Eight, leading industrialised nations (G8) in 1999 to call for renewed commitment of all partners to lifelong learning: "... by governments, investing to enhance education and training at all levels; by the private sector, training existing and future employees; by individuals, developing their own abilities and careers." However, structural adjustment programmes, restrictive fiscal policies, low wages, debt repayment obligations, decline of development assistance flows, competitive price pressures on enterprises and lack of resources of large sections of the population in a number of cases induce governments, enterprises and individuals to under-invest in education and training. Furthermore, market uncertainties, poaching of skills by other enterprises and the growth of insecure forms of work and consequential high turnover of staff may reduce enterprises' incentives to invest in training. This is especially true for the least developed countries, most of which are in Africa, given their dire socio-economic situation. The culture of developing, on a continuous basis, individual and collective skills for enhanced productivity and employability in a rapidly changing environment has to be improved further.

11. The cost of education and training should be seen as an investment. Increasing this investment can be fostered by recognising that investing in education and training can

be a shared responsibility of both the public and private sector. Government must always assume the primary responsibility for investing in basic education and initial training, and it should also invest in other forms of training. Government must also share the greatest responsibility for investments directed at groups where combating social exclusion or discrimination is an important objective. With respect to the responsibility of individuals, the government must also share responsibility in order that access not be denied on financial grounds and to the detriment of the broader interest of society. Government, as an employer, must also assume responsibility to invest in training. With respect to the private sector, the responsibilities of both enterprises and individuals should be recognised and, where appropriate, encouraged. These responsibilities are especially appropriate with respect to investment in workplace-based and continuous education, which can raise workers' employability and the competitiveness of enterprises. The organisation and implementation of private sector responsibilities in this area can best be accomplished through partnerships between the government and enterprises, between government and the social partners or between the social partners. Ensuring increased investment for SMEs is especially suitable to a partnership approach.

12. There is no universal model of investing in training. Governments should create a general economic environment and incentives conducive to encourage individuals and enterprises to invest individually or jointly in education and training. This investment and the responsibility for it should generally be determined by the objectives of training, e.g., individual, enterprise or societal objectives. Countries can use different ways and means to foster investment in training and increase resources for training. Enterprises have a critical role to play in investment in training. A number of mechanisms

used in combination to further investment in training and to guarantee access are required. These may include levy systems on enterprises accompanied by public grants, establishment of training funds, various incentives for training and learning, e.g., tax rebates, training credits, training awards, individual training accounts, collective and individual training rights, sabbatical leave, collective training agreements and emulation of national and international best practices of investing in training. The chosen mechanisms should take into account the special needs of the SMEs. Where levies are the chosen mechanism for funding training, the governance of funding distribution should be tripartite, or where these are agreed by the social partners, such governance should be bipartite. Decisions regarding government policies on education and training should be based on genuine tripartite dialogue and give the tripartite partners the opportunity to develop the best ways and means to increase investments in training. Measures such as the provision of child-care facilities are needed to facilitate access to training. One means of encouraging countries and companies to increase current efforts possibly differentiated for different regions of the world, size of companies or sector of industry, as a mirror and point of orientation for countries, sectors, and companies.

13. Flatter hierarchical structures, and devolved decision making, initiative and control, also widen the need for higher-level skills and training, and result in increased responsibility for workers. ICT is accelerating these management trends and changes in the world of work in general. It has the potential to improve enormously people's access to quality education and training, including in the workplace. There is however a danger that these technologies may create a "digital divide" and worsen existing inequalities in education and training between urban and rural areas, between rich and poor, between those who possess and those who lack literacy and

numeracy skills, and between developed and developing countries. Countries should expand their investment in the infrastructure needed for use of ICT, in education and training hardware and software, and in the training of teachers and trainers. Such investments should be undertaken by both the public and private sectors, and make use of collaborative local, national and international networks. Governments may also provide incentives for the private sector and individuals to encourage computer literacy and to develop new communication skills. New modes and methods need to be deployed for training and learning when using ICT. Distance-learning methods can be used to make training available at convenient times, at accessible places or at reduced costs. Distance learning should not replace all other learning or teaching methods but can be a valuable part of the total teaching tools available. Distance learning should, as far as possible, be combined with traditional training methods in order to avoid a sense of isolation of the learner. The social framework for training needs to be adapted to these new forms of training.

14. The many driving forces have a significant impact on organisation and working methods of companies. Also, new sectors are emerging, many of them based on the use of ICT products and services, including the internet. All this increases demand for new skills and competencies, including personal skills and ICT competencies. Education and training need to respond to these new demands, both those related to ICT and those related to changing work organisation.

15. Electronic networking provides opportunities for learners to assist each other more actively, for learners to be more active in the training and education process, and for formal and non-conventional teaching methods to be utilised. In order to apply ICT in training, trainers must master these technologies and be systematically trained. Teaching methods need to be updated to accommodate the

teaching of new developments in ICT, new types of organisation of schools should be devised to take full advantage of ICT; and the individual needs to learn self-learning methods. New training is needed to provide trainers and individuals with these skills. Enterprises may provide ICT facilities or support schemes for workers for the use of ICT at home or in general, and to schools or other training providers, in order to promote the diffusion of ICT skills and access in society. Appropriate government incentives could facilitate this development.

16. For many developing countries, the challenges are much more basic. Societies with huge and growing levels of adult illiteracy, and massive debt crises, will not be able to design, fund or implement the modern education and training policies which are prerequisites for development and economic growth. In the age of the knowledge society, 884 million adults are illiterate, unable to operate effectively even with the intellectual tools of the "old economy". UNESCO estimates that, in the least developed countries, while 144 million adults were illiterate in 1985, by 2005 this will rise to 188 million – in other words, the number of illiterate adults will grow by 30 per cent in the least developed countries. Additionally, structural adjustment programmes have in specific instances operated to reduce public investment in education, thus further weakening the longer term capacity for economic growth and development.

Much of the developing world lacks access to the physical infrastructure through which much of the new knowledge is pulsing. The lack of electricity and telephones, the cost of computers and internet access, all contribute to deprive citizens, enterprises and workers in developing countries from benefiting from the ICT revolution, and create the conditions for a "digital divide" to grow between countries. Developing countries should make greater efforts to invest in ICT and to develop ICT-appropriate methods of teaching rather than simply adding computers to existing teaching methods. The international community should, as part of creating the conditions for skills formation in the least developed economies, undertake bold and substantial debt relief, or, where appropriate, debt cancellation; help mobilise resources for programmes to secure basic literacy and numeracy and the development of communication and information infrastructure; and assist with training in the new information and communication technologies. This is a direct challenge to the ILO and international development agencies.

Multinational corporations should be encouraged to agree fair technology transfer agreements, to develop local high-level skills in developing countries, and to help create the infrastructure for the new knowledge economy. The contributions to development that multinational companies can make through training as elaborated in the Tripartite Declaration of Principles concerning Multinational Enterprises and Social Policy should be recalled. These measures, taken together, contribute to developing thc cconomies and societies of the poorest parts of the world. They provide a ladder through which developing countries can move up the value chain in production, making goods and providing services which add significant economic value, and which receive significant economic return in the global economy. Education and training is one of the packages of measures to leapfrog from underdevelopment to the information society.

In developing an education and training base in developing countries, the existence of new technology can open up new possibilities and possibly save costs on more traditional methods. This is a major challenge for the developing countries to invest in ICT and develop appropriate policies.

Closer collaboration is needed between the ILO, UNESCO and other international organisations; regional organisations, such as the EU and MERCOSUR; and donor countries that place high priority on human resources development and training. It should also work more closely with international financial institutions such as the International Monetary Fund, the World Bank, and regional development banks, to ensure that structural adjustment programmes do not inhibit investments in education and training. Greater national and international efforts also should be made to eradicate illiteracy worldwide. All of these measures and support can only be effective if the developing countries make efforts to set up policies and programmes to promote economic growth and develop their human talent.

17. The development of a national qualifications framework is in the interest of enterprises and workers as it facilitates lifelong learning, helps enterprises and employment agencies match skill demand with supply, and guides individuals in their choice of training and career. The framework should consist of a number of elements: appropriate, transferable, broad and industry-based and professional competency standards, established by the social partners, that reflect the skills required in the economy and public institutions, and vocational and academic qualifications; and a credible, fair and transparent system of assessment of skills learned and competencies gained, irrespective of how and where they have been learned, e.g., through formal and non-formal education and training, work experience and on-the-job learning. Every person should have the opportunity to have his or her experiences and skills gained through work, through society or through formal and non-formal training assessed, recognised and certified. Programmes to compensate for skill deficits by individuals through increased access to education and training should be made available as part of recognition of prior learning programmes. Assessment should identify skill gaps, be transparent, and provide a guide to the learner and

training provider. The framework should also include a credible system of certification of skills that are portable and recognised across enterprises, sectors, industries and educational institutions, whether public or private.

The assessment methodology should be fair, linked to standards, and be non-discriminatory. Potential hidden discrimination should be actively guarded against. For example, the shift to the service sector, with an overall stronger female component, often relies on greater communication and problem-solving skills, which are not always explicitly recognised. Similarly, testing systems conducted in an individual's second language sometimes distort results of technical and other skills possessed. New forms of work organisation often shift the skills requirements within an enterprise. For example, flatter managerial structures are predicated on shifting certain responsibilities from management to the workforce. These should result in explicit recognition of the new competencies required by the workforce under these circumstances; and reward systems have to take these into account.

The vocational qualifications system should be tripartite, offer access to workers and anybody wanting to learn, should cover public and private training providers and be updated on a continuous basis. It should ensure multiple entry and exit points in the education and training system during a worker's career. The ILO should develop a database on best practices in developing a national qualifications framework, conduct a general study on the comparability of different national qualifications frameworks based on this database, and undertake research into recognition of prior learning.

18. Trade unions and employer associations may also contribute to training by managing their own training institutions and providing education for their members. Particularly at the sector and enterprise levels, collective

bargaining can set appropriate conditions for the organisation and implementation of training. Such collective bargaining could encompass issues such as:

a) skills required by the enterprise and the economy;
b) training necessary for workers;
c) assessment of basic skills and skills gained either in the workplace or during individual or associative activities;
c) development of career paths for workers;
d) personal training and development plans for workers;
e) facilities needed to allow the maximum benefits from training; and
f) recognition and reward schemes, including remuneration structuring.

19. The social partners should strengthen social dialogue on training, share responsibility in formulating education and training policies, and engage in partnerships with each other or with governments for investing in, planning and implementing training. In training, networks of cooperation also include regional and local government, various ministries, sector and professional bodies, training institutions and providers, non-governmental organisations, etc. Government should establish a framework for effective social dialogue and partnerships in training and employment. This should result in a coordinated education and training policy at the national level, and long-term strategies, which are formulated in consultation with the social partners and are integrated with economic and employment policies. It should also include tripartite, national and sector training arrangements, and provide for a transparent and comprehensive training and labour market information system. Enterprises are primarily responsible for training their employees and apprentices, but also share responsibility in initial vocational training of young people to meet their future needs.

20. The scope and effectiveness of social dialogue and partnerships in training is currently limited by the capacity and resources of actors. It varies between countries, sectors and large and small enterprises. Recent regional economic integration also brings a new dimension to social dialogue on training and the need for capacity building. There is a pressing need to raise this capacity by various means such as technical cooperation, public grants to trade union and employer organisations, and exchanging experience and best practices between countries. Education and training in industrial relations and on trade union education, business administration and the social contribution by the work and the organisation of the social partners, should also be an integral part of capacity building and a part of initial and vocational training. Being a tripartite organisation, the ILO should lead international cooperation to build up capacities for social dialogue and partnership building in training. Additional efforts should be made for the benefit of developing countries.

21. Terms of reference for a review of the Human Resources Development Recommendation, 1975 should be based on the present conclusions, adopted by the International Labour Conference at its 88th Session, 2000, the conclusions of the Cologne Charter 1999, and the statements on this subject jointly made by international employer and trade union organisations; and should include the following:

    i) address training and education needs in the modern world of work in both developing and developed countries, and promote social equity in the global economy;

    ii) advance the decent work concept through defining the role of education and training;

    iii) promote lifelong learning, enhance employability of the world's workers, and address the economic challenges;

iv) recognise the various responsibilities for investment and funding of education and training;.

v) promote national, regional and international qualifications frameworks which include provisions for prior learning;

vi) improve access and equity of opportunity for all workers to education and training;

viii)build the capacity of the social partners for partnerships in education and training;

ix) address the need for increased technical and financial assistance for the less advantaged countries and societies.

Recommendation No. 150 should be revised in order to reflect the new approach to training. Although some aspects of the Recommendation are still valid, others have lost their relevance. There is a need for a more dynamic instrument that is more applicable and used by member states and the social partners in formulating and implementing human resources development policies, integrated with other economic and social policies, particularly employment policies. A new recommendation should be complemented by a practical guide and database that can be renewed on a continuous basis by the office as part of its normal work.

REFERENCES

Blanksby, V., P. Bruhn, "Technical and Vocational Education in Australia", *UNEVOC*, 1995

Delailomaloma, N. H., "Technical and Vocational Education and Training in Fiji", *UNEVOC,* 1995.

Friberg, N., B. Carnstam, "The Role of Technical and Vocational Education in the Swedish Education System", *UNEVOC*, 1995.

King, K., *Aid and Education in the Developing World*, 1992.

Neudorf, R., "Diagnosis of the Estonian Vocational Education System: Indicators for Evaluation and Monitoring", *Unesco, Paris, IIEP*, 1994.

4

Technologies in Education: Challenges and Responses

Vocational education and training (VOCED) has been in the past, is today, and will remain in the future one of the hottest debated subjects in all countries of the world. Among the several reasons for this phenomenon is the close intuitive link between VOCED and technological development. If technology is seen as a panacea for modernising a country's economy and achieving higher levels of per capita income, the next logical step is to instil into the labour force the 'necessary skills' for such higher technology to be applied and further developed. But there are still other reasons for the recurrent popularity of VOCED in policy discussions.

This type of education is being perceived to be par excellence to social engineering. Just as you can build a bridge to lower transportation costs between two sides of a river, so by providing vocational education a country can allegedly prosper economically and reap more easily the benefits of economic growth. VOCED is also seen as a possible policy instrument to keep unemployed youth out of city streets, in the hope that it would help them, sometime, to find useful employment.

It has been provided to poor segments of the population as a means to raising their income. It has been offered as a viable option to those primary or secondary school students who are being judged unable to pursue academic studies, 'so that they will have acquired a useful skill' when moving to adult life. And the recent expansion of trade liberalisation and economic globalisation have naturally trickled down to their implications for VOCED.

TRADITIONAL APPROACH

Although it is hard to generalise, given the great diversity of VOCED's organisation, financing and delivery modes in different countries, the following common/typical features are bound to strike a familiar chord. VOCED is called upon to solve multiple, sometimes conflicting objectives, some of which had better been dealt with by other types of policies, completely unrelated to education and training. Several illustrations occur. The following are some alternative and complementary solutions:

i) *Youth unemployment*: Not all young people find immediate employment as soon as they graduate from school or a training programme. A common remedy often proposed is to offer them VOCED. This, allegedly, would kill two birds with one stone: take the youth off the streets, and at the same time equip them with skills that could be used later in the labour market.

ii) *Instilling technological knowledge*: Starting from the British Industrial Revolution, followed up by Germany and Japan in this century, it is a common belief that economic progress heavily depends on technological know-how. The next logical step in this reasoning is that VOCED must expand.

iii) *Academically less able students*: There has always been concern with a great number of students who 'are not able' to advance through the school system, especially the academic stream of secondary education. Hence, the provision of VOCED to them would allegedly equip them with something useful to do later in life.

iv) *Lack of middle level technicians*: There is no country in the world where a number of specialities are not in 'scarce' supply (e.g., plumbers and nurses). So the next logical reasoning is that such skills in short supply should be created by the country's vocational schools and training institutions.

v) *Poverty among urban dwellers*: A more modern variant of the above themes is that, given the increased poverty of urban dwellers, the provision of VOCED would give useful skills to the unemployed and make them find productive employment and thus raise their income.

vi) *Economic globalisation*: Given the fact that frontiers have expanded by means of freer trade and multinationals, this development has to have implications on the nature of VOCED received by the labour force. Neither has the expansion of VOCED solved the youth unemployment problem, nor have less academically able students been persuaded to abandon their striving to follow academic courses and enter the university, let alone has urban poverty been mitigated.

Sociologists, psychologists (and economists, to some extent) have amply documented that it is pointless to try to change through schooling or training deeply embedded family values and aspirations. A student from an upper income family will always strive towards secondary education and eventually enter the university. Even farmers have boycotted the so-called 'ruralised curricula' (vocationalisation at the lowest level) because they have observed social dynamics and know that such kind of education would hamper the chances of their offspring moving to the city where the best opportunities are.

The shortage of certain skills, ironically, might have little to do with the availability of VOCED. Such shortage might be an artefact of, for example, a centrally set wage rate making people unwilling to serve as nurses or plumbers. Revising the salary structure to correspond more closely to that in the free market would eliminate such shortages overnight. Or, even if in the presence of a skill shortage the number of graduates in that occupation were increased, there is no guarantee that such graduates would work in the intended occupation.

The literature is full of examples of graduates from secondary vocational schools who eventually work in diametrically opposite occupation, mostly clerical. Of course, technology and VOCED are closely linked. But it is easily forgotten that, given rapid technological change, the best VOCED might be general education and training. This is not as paradoxical as it sounds, because general education allows a person to be more easily trainable than one who was trained in a narrow set of skills.

Delivery Mechanisms in Training Technologies

Group learning may take place in a local or remote (supposing travel and possibly lodging) classroom or auditorium, or via distance learning. When the learners and the teacher are not in the same room, the learners are geographically spread and follow the course live with the possibility to interact as if they were in a classroom; one speaks then about virtual classroom. The classroom is the usual learning environment for many people in the world. It has undoubtedly irreplaceable advantages:

i) having a live teacher in the class offers a great deal of interaction (between teacher and learners, but also between learners themselves), the possibility to have personal attention (if the number of learners is reasonable) and also to get an immediate answer to the learners' questions;

ii) possibility to use all senses (hearing, sight, touch, smell, taste), to organise group discussions, role-playing or hands-on exercises, to learn by doing;

iii) the development and update cycle is shorter for a classroom course than for any other form of delivery discussed hereafter;

But it also has limitations:

i) if learners are dispersed geographically, the same course has to be given by several teachers in different places, or alternatively the teacher or the learners have to travel (travel and lodging expenses); and

ii) the class size is seldom the right one: too many learners in the class, or too few to justify the course;

iii) the learners have to follow the course when it is offered; this is particularly constraining in continuous education, where the course may be offered too late or too early.

The classroom may be local, i.e., the course is given close to the place where the learners live, or remote, i.e., the teacher and/or the leaners have to travel and stay in another location for the course length in a residential training centre.

In the distance learning environment, the teacher and the learners are not at the same location, sometimes even very far from each other. The course is given once, at a certain location, and broadcast to many locations. The important characteristic of this approach is that the classroom conditions are reproduced, even if sometimes in a limited way. Broadcasting may happen in two ways:

i) the teacher delivers the course in a classroom (sometimes called "candid classroom"), with some learners in it, and the broadcasting equipment is used by a specialised crew. In this case, the teacher does not take care of the transmission and teaches as usual. However, the teacher should learn how to behave in front of a camera and how to prepare visuals for a good transmission. This may be convenient for improving teachers' presentation skills.

ii) the teacher may also be trained to use the equipment of a studio from which the course is delivered. No learners will be physically, attending the course in this case, no specialised crew is around, only a technical support. This is a good approach for teachers who are technology-oriented and will use this system regularly.

On the reception side, the course may be followed live or deferred:

i) if followed live, the learners watch the course on a screen or TV monitor at their location and may interrupt the teacher, who normally does not see them, with a feature sometimes called "student-response unit". The system does not only allow an audio interruption but allows learners to answer multiple questions shown by the teacher on the screen. The results of all locations are consolidated and shown to all. The teacher has a view of how the learners are following and may decide to go on or to return to topics not well understood;

ii) if the course is followed in a deferred mode, it is first recorded on videotapes and later watched by small groups of learners, if possible with the help of a tutor or facilitator who answers questions, clarifies some topics, gives homework, etc. Distance learning has its own limitations, specially when used in deferred mode:

iii) interaction is limited;

iv) hands-on training is difficult and role-playing is practically impossible to organise;

v) not all senses can be used, only sight and hearing;

vi) development and update cycles are longer than for a classroom course, because the developers have to think carefully to present everything in a way that can be understood remotely, with possible interaction and feedback; and

viii) learners may need more time to master the course content, because they have to rely more on themselves; this is particularly true for those who are used to learning with a permanent supervision.

Individual learning (also called 'self-study') has a number of advantages, even more when considering continuing education:

i) the learner proceeds at his or her own pace, may review part or all of the course as many times as necessary, anywhere and any time;

ii) training is provided, if possible, on a demand basis, not on an offer basis, and is available, if possible, at any place, any time;

iii) training is provided in a consistent manner; all learners will receive the same messages expressed exactly in the same way;

iv) learning time may be reduced according to the learner's previous knowledge of the subject, learning skills, preferred learning styles; and

v) more attractive courses are offered, based on new concepts (multimedia, hypermedia), so learners follow them with more motivation, and the result is an increased retention rate.

But it has of course some limitations:

i) development and update cycles are considerably longer than for a classroom course on the same subject, making it not very suitable for subjects having a short life expectancy, or needing frequent updates;

ii) it cannot easily be used to learn subjects like human relationship, affective behaviours, selling skills, confidence building, corporate culture, etc., although some experiences have been made with a certain success; and

iii) it cannot be used by learners who need to be regularly supervised by another person.

The technological evolution of personal computers, as well as their decreasing price, allow more and more people to have a PC at home, which they can use for CAL in addition to their other preferred activities (accounting, playing games, etc.). Programmes provided by the teachers, or bought off-the-shelf from publishers (language courses, basic courses in mathematics, electronics, etc.) facilitate computer-assisted learning. PCs, working in a stand-alone mode or in LAN, are also used at the workplace; learners can use their own workstation, or those installed in a learning centre, which is sometimes organised within the company or outside, by a group of companies or a professional association.

When PCs are available at the workplace to provide training when needed, one speaks -about "just-in-ime-training". It allows access to training at the moment it is required and at the time at which the learner has to put his or her knowledge into practice. CAL courseware, tutorials, online help, data bases, etc., may be available on the user's workstation, or via a network. It also allows one to reduce the basic training time, by eliminating commuting and waiting time to attend courses if and when they are available. This approach is sometimes referred to as Electronic Performance Support System (EPSS).

Soft Technologies

New approaches are being progressively implemented, which may deeply change the way we learn, and which we would call "soft technologies". Hypertext (or hypermedia, when more than just text is involved) is the first example of such technologies. It might change the traditional way of learning which is:

a) linear, sequential, very "directive",
b) the same for every leaner (whatever his or her learning style, previous knowledge, available time, etc.), and
c) hardly interactive (a programme can hardly be labelled interactive if it only offers a selection from a menu).

The hypertext or hypermedia offers a way of "navigating" in the subject matter, closer to a personal, empirical and exploratory way of learning. The educational role of hypertext and hypermedia is nevertheless not recognised by everybody. It is considered more as an information tool, a discovery system, because the links between objects are difficult to control and may lead to wrong associations. The leaner may never be sure of having seen or learned the whole subject. One can of course use, after having explored the subject matter, a knowledge verification system, but such an evaluation programme is seldom offered in hypertexts.

Intelligent tutoring systems, an improvement of traditional CAL courseware based on the introduction of artificial intelligence (Al), is probably the future individual learning system. At the moment it exists on a research and prototype basis. An intelligent tutoring system progressively builds and updates a learner's model, and adjusts the way one uses the programme to his or her model detected via the man-machine interaction (questions, answers, errors, etc.).

This is certainly not yet totally ready for implementation on a large scale, but more work is being done which opens very interesting prospects. Courses developed this way are necessarily more expensive, because their design is considerably complex. However, the result expected should be so greatly rewarding that it is worth thc cffort. Another approach has been recently implemented, which can help develop and update courses faster and cheaper.

The subject matter, which is embedded in the course structure and organisation in a traditional CAL, is "atomised" in a separate database (called "knowledge base") which means that it can be used for different courses, by different people, and be updated in a central place. Courses update in this way is made much simpler and cheaper. The implementation is too recent to judge the approach. The remark expressed about Al-based courseware also applies here: longer and more complex design and development, but much better results expected with regard to learning quality.

Virtual reality (VR) is another concept which is still at the research stage for training applications, but which is very promising for certain aspects of learning. It requires very powerful and expensive work stations, at least if one wishes to take full advantage of the so-called fully immersive VR. Flight simulators in training pilots use some concepts of VR. A limited version now exists for high-end PCs, called the "desktop VR". For training, virtual reality will most probably be particularly powerful in the area of 3D simulation.

The learner will no longer change parameters with the keyboard or the mouse, but will really (or better, virtually) walk into the system or room, turning knobs, touching objects, which offers an almost perfect realism. VR software currently offered on the market implies quite a bit of additional programming (e.g., in C++ language) which not everybody is likely to afford.

On top of that, VR supposes the use of rather expensive equipment: special gloves, helmets with built-in small screens for every eye, 2D/3D mice, etc. But prices will decrease as progress is made, which seems to go rather quickly. Another aspect of VR that might be interesting for training is the possibility, via networks, to have several persons working remotely but simultaneously at a VR application, the possibility of generating 3D group work in real time!

REFERENCES

Drake, K., "Interventions in market financing of training in the European Community", in Ryan, P. (ed.), *International comparisons of vocational education and training for intermediate skills*, The Falmer Press, 1991.

______________ , Germe, J. F., "Financing continuing training: What are the lessons from international comparison?" *Berlin: CEDEFOP*, 1995.

Dougherty, C., "The cost-effectiveness of national training systems in developing countries", *PPR Working Paper Series*, WPS 171, Washington, D.C.: World Bank, 1989.

Gasskov, V., *Alternative schemes of financial training*, Geneva: ILO, 1994.

Gomes, C., "Alternatives in vocational education finance: an example of participation by employers in Brazil", *Training and discussion papers*, No. 69, Geneva: ILO, 1991.

5

Assessment and Appropriate Technologies in TVE

The priority in assessment in the past—whether in the classroom or in large-scale public examination—has been for forms which compared individuals with each other. In vocational education, however, assessment needs to be thought of not as a comparison between individuals, but as "the process of collecting evidence and making judgments on the extent and nature of progress towards the performance requirements set out in a standard, or a learning outcome." Despite frequent claims, this has rarely been the case. Particular problems have been:

i) assessment of students on those matters which it is easy to assess, leading to an overemphasis on memory and lower level skills.

ii) assessment encouraging students to focus on those topics which are assessed at the expense of those which are not.

iii) students giving precedence to graded assessment tasks over those which are ungraded.

iv) students adopting undesirable approaches to learning influenced by the nature of assessment tasks.

v) students retaining fundamental misconceptions about key concepts in the subjects they have passed, despite performing well in examinations.

vi) successful students seeking cues from teachers to enable them to identify what is important for formal assessment purposes, and consequently ignoring important but unassessed material.

As a result, existing assessment approaches can have quite the opposite effects to those desired. Fortunately, the issue of the links between competence, learning and assessment has now come to prominence, and it is possible to look afresh at ways in which assessment can fulfil two necessary requirements: that it measures competence, and that it has a beneficial effect on the learning process.

Assessment is the most significant prompt for learning: every act of assessment gives a message to students about what they should be learning and how they should go about it. The message is often not explicit, is not easily understood and often it is read differently and is often given a different emphasis by teachers and by students. Good assessment is not just a matter of finding the "appropriate" method and using it sensibly in conjunction with given subject matter. There are always unintended consequences in assessment.

Students will learn to adopt "surface" approaches to study in some circumstances, and will adopt "deep" approaches in others. In so doing, they will be prompted partly by the forms and nature of assessment tasks. They will learn that, in order to maximise their marks, they should use rote learning in many circumstances, even when the teacher might believe that this would distract them from the most important aspects of the course. This response—and other undesirable ones—will be a function not only of the assessment tasks set, but also of all the experiences of assessment students have had in the past. If, for example, they get the idea that memorisation works for multiple-choice tests, they will persist in that strategy even when assured that it will not help.

Students are not simply responding to the given subject. They carry with them the totality of their experiences of learning and being assessed and this certainly extends far beyond concurrent and immediately preceding subjects. All of this means that the way a student approaches the task of learning will depend on:

a) the intrinsic qualities of the form of assessment being used;
b) the ways in which the assessor translates the material to be assessed into the given format, and selects assessment tasks appropriate for the subject and the specific learning goals; and
c) (most importantly) how the student interprets the task at hand and the context of the assessment.

The latter interpretation does not only depend on the form of the assessment process, but on how these tasks are embedded within the total context of the subject and within the total experience of the course and of the student's life. For instance, assessment tasks are set by experienced, often well educated, professional educators with a deep subject knowledge, for inexperienced learners who are often from a different generation and possibly a different culture. These major differences must inevitably affect the interpretation of any assessed tasks.

Students also experience the interaction effects of one form of assessment on another. In one month they may have to complete ten assessment tasks, in another month only one. The ways in which they approach each of these will be influenced by the others. A task which is intrinsically interesting and which may be approached meaningfully at any other time may be given short shrift when it is located among a thicket of assessments. Very little attention has been given to the compounding effects of assessment, even when teachers know that it is the total array of demands in a given period which influences how each one is tackled.

An issue that has not received enough attention is how to best use the capacities and skills of students to assess themselves. This is of greater long-term significance than the effect of any specific subject-matter learning. Students must leave a vocational education course equipped to engage in self-assessment throughout their professional lives. They need to be able to make reliable judgements about what they know and do not know, and what they can and cannot do.

Too often staff-driven assessment encourages students to be dependent on the teacher or the examiners to make decisions about what they know, and they do not effectively learn to do this for themselves. At present, students learn most about self-assessment through their own informal second-guessing of their performance on the assessment tasks which are set, but this is rarely adequate. A variety of ways of giving practice to students in self-assessment is required. In particular, self-assessment activities, in which students learn to distinguish acceptable from unacceptable performance, need to be developed, and self-assessment actively encouraged.

A starting-point for doing this is:

i) clarifying the concept of criteria in terms with which the students are familiar, for example, by asking "how would you distinguish good work from poor work in this subject?"

ii) spelling out the criteria In sufficient detail to make it possible for each student to make a judgement on the extent to which the criteria have been met. The criteria need to specify

a) the area to be assessed

b) the aims of the assessed work

c) the standards to be reached.

Strategies then need to be put in place to assist the self-assessment process. The two most common are the use of written schedules, and structured group activities.

Appropriate Technologies

The decision to use one or more NTTs, and which ones, is

essential because once the decision has been taken it will have an impact on the teaching/learning process for many years. Selecting NTTs becomes one small part of an educational system's approach which will focus on what education and training to offer to whom, where, when, how and why. Among the suggested approaches, one starts with a needs' analysis: how many people do we need to educate or train, for what skills. The needs analysis may be based on national or regional development planning, on projections for business and industry for the next few years, or on the business targets for a specific company. It results in training goals.

Clearly defined objectives help to establish performance requirements which, compared to the current level of knowledge and skills, indicate precisely the training requirements. The analysis of the training requirements results in a curriculum, divided into courses or modules. For each module, the decision about how to deliver it has to be taken and then, but only then, the use of NTTs may be considered. To close the process loop, one has to set up in place measurement and evaluation systems in order to be able to verify whether the objectives have been reached.

When looking at the delivery mechanism to be used for a course or for a particular course module, three steps may be identified:

i) a political or strategic decision to use or not to use some NTTs for education and training needs to be taken from the outset;
ii) if the decision is "yes, we wish to use NTTs", a non-quantitative analysis of the education and training environment will help to select either group or individual learning;
iii) a quantitative analysis ("cost model") will then be applied to the selected delivery mechanism in order to decide whether the training material will be bought off-the-shelf, custom developed or developed in-house and what type of NTTs should be considered.

Political or strategic decision has to be taken at the national or regional level by the highest authorities in charge of education and training, at management level for business concerns. Taking the right decision implies a serious analysis of needs, target population, existing resources and to be well informed about the most recent NTT applications, advantages, limitations and costs.

Decision making requires access to a network of updated information, success stories, demonstrations, and exchange of ideas with professionals. The decision to use NTTs implies that appropriate measures need to be taken to make the necessary resources available (money, people, equipment); and to provide the trainers in charge of the implementation with appropriate training. The availability of technologies in a certain place at a certain point in time is another essential parameter, and of course the availability of funds and the political willingness to invest in NTTs.

Cost/Benefit Assessment

Once the delivery mechanism has been selected, decision makers are confronted with the choice between:

a) buying the training material off-the-shelf;
b) contacting an external institution or company to develop it (custom development); and
c) developing it in the institution or company itself (in-house development).

This decision is based on a cost/benefit analysis, or a cost model. Costs and benefits should be analysed at different levels: courseware development, learning material distribution, education delivery and update are the most important ones. Intangible costs and benefits should not be neglected, because they may be very important in a certain number of situations. For each stage of the learning material development, distribution, delivery and update, different types of costs and benefits have to be considered: personnel costs (salaries of developers, teachers but also learners when already at work, travel and living expenses), equipment costs (computer hardware and software, telecommunications, audio and video equipment) and others (e.g., buildings).

Having analysed the development and distribution costs, one should not neglect the delivery costs which may be very substantial and influence the final decision. The personnel costs may represent a significant percentage of the total delivery cost: the number of teaching (and/or tutoring) hours multiplied by the cost per hour.

When learners are at work, their salary during training time is an important factor, on top of the fact that they are not productive during that period. Trainers may have to repeat the same course to different groups of employees. Travel and living expenses may be very heavy if learners are geographically spread in a big country or region. The choice of the appropriate NTTs may considerably decrease travel and living expenses of both teachers and learners, which may represent appreciable savings. Then come the infrastructure and equipment costs.

If classrooms or an auditorium are not available, the cost of building or renting them should be considered. If computers and computer networks have to be installed, their cost should be considered, as well as the cost of their use (telecommunications, leased lines, satellite broadcasting time, etc.). If courses are based on multimedia courseware, some equipment will be necessary to use them. However, NTTs hardware costs should be considered as an investment, not as an expense as it is too frequently the case. NTTs will be depreciated over several years as are the other investments (buildings, class and laboratory equipment, etc.).

A new approach to assessment is already espoused in previous pages, in which the emphasis is on demonstrated competence rather than on comparisons with others, and in which students' skills and knowledge can be recognised, regardless of how or where they were attained. When large numbers of students across many institutions need to be assessed, however, there is a difficulty in adopting these ideas. With regard to the connection between assessment and learning, whilst the form of assessment can have a very powerful effect on the way students choose to learn, there is none of the interchange between teacher and student which makes formative assessment such a powerful aid to learning. With regard to assessment and competence, there are many desirable aspects of assessment of competence which are impractical to implement across many institutions, with our current state of understanding.

That is, there is a problem in measuring students' competence in the abstract and removed from the context in which it is to be applied, within a structure that normally requires a fixed time limit for all and a particular selection of areas to be tested. However, large-scale assessment procedures are often carried out in many countries, where they are seen as the best way of ensuring uniformity of standards. It refers to a situation in which assessment is both summative and "external", and the assessment system may be operated by an authority which administers and controls a regional or national system for educational or training institutions.

Formative assessment, on the other hand, is inevitably left to the colleges and other training institutions, where it occurs as part of the teaching programme. External assessment authorities are likely to have highly organised procedures for processing assessments and detailed operational systems which can cope with a wide range of eventualities, some of which may only rarely occur. Such authorities often respond to and reflect national policies on education and training and may be accountable to government. External assessment systems provide information to the principal stakeholders: students, teachers and those who make decisions about selecting for employment, further or higher education or training.

External assessment within large systems will generally be carried out by an external assessment board, normally an agency completely independent of all the colleges in which students are enrolled. The goal of such boards is to provide valid and reliable, high-quality public examinations, tests and related services at low cost to educational, training, industrial and commercial organisations within their national jurisdiction. Within the system of assessment there will be those components which are administered externally by such a board and marked by examiners trained and controlled by it. These will generally be unseen written examinations or tests.

Other assessment components might be set centrally but assessed by the candidates' or students' own teachers, or trainers. External assessment systems throughout the world normally use a combination of examiner-marked and teacher-marked assessments. Authorities responsible for administering external assessments operate in the public domain, are under close scrutiny, and are usually monitored and regulated by government.

Whether the organisation is a company or a government agency, it will have to operate on a cost-effective basis with technically sound assessments which make realistic demands on the organisation's own administration and that of the examination centres it serves. The assessments should meet the needs of all types of students seeking qualifications at any given level and meet the needs of a nation's social, economic and political imperatives.

The administration system should ensure that candidates' results are accurate and fair and are issued on time. Administrative rules relating to a variety of situations will be needed, for example, whether any candidates will be refused admission, prohibited combinations of subjects, acceptance of late entries, policy on refund of fees for withdrawals, transfer of candidates between centres, special arrangements for candidates with special needs, and arrangements for candidates who are absent from part of an assessment due to illness.

Competence

Traditional approaches to assessment have assumed that intelligence is distributed in a regular fashion represented by the normal curve. This assumption underpins much of the way in which people have thought about assessment, and the generation of such measures as percentile ranks. Tests based on these assumptions seek to differentiate between individuals-that is, to find out where individuals fit in this distribution represented by the normal curve. Thus questions or items are selected in this measurement model of assessment on the basis of how well they discriminate between people. That is, excellence is determined by how well individuals perform relative to others. If all candidates performed well in the test, its constructors would assume it was a bad test—not that all the students performed excellently.

Assumptions of the standards-based model are quite different. They are that educational standards can be set, most students can achieve them, different performances can reflect the same standards, and assessors can judge these performances consistently. The use of such a model affects the approach to both training and assessment which is currently being implemented in vocational education in many countries Courses are designed and delivery undertaken to achieve the specified standards, and assessment is based on these standards. Tests based on this model are informed by public standards and seek to measure students' understanding of the processes and concepts that underpin performance in authentic settings such as the workplace.

Such tests become vital learning tools, and can be carried out at various times over a school or college year. Students need not necessarily achieve standards at the same time, so evidence may be gathered over time using a variety of methods and in various contexts. Reliability issues are approached not by objective scoring methods but by the use of professional judgement and the use of exemplars. Assessors become "judges", weighing evidence and assessing how well performances reflect defined standards.

A competency-based approach to assessment is highly appropriate to vocational education and training:

i) to ensure that teaching and assessment serve the required outcomes, rather than being based, for example, on courses undertaken or time served.

ii) to facilitate the granting of credit for competency acquired elsewhere.

iii) to help students clearly understand what is expected of them if they are to succeed in the course.

iv) to -inform potential employers what a particular qualification means.

The basic principles of assessment are that it should be valid, reliable, flexible and fair:

i) *Validity*: Assessments are valid when they assess what they claim to assess. This is achieved when:

a) assessors are fully aware of what is to be assessed (against some appropriate criterion or defined learning outcome)

b) evidence is collected from tasks that are clearly related to what is to be assessed

c) there is enough sampling of different evidence to demonstrate that the performance criterion has been met.

ii) *Reliability*: Assessments are reliable when they are applied and interpreted consistently from student to student, and from one context to another.

iii) *Flexibility*: Assessments are flexible when they are successfully adapted to a range of training modes and the different needs of different learners.

iv) *Fairness*: Assessments are fair when they do not disadvantage particular learners-for example, when all learners understand what is expected of them and what form an assessment will take.

Under a competency-based assessment system, assessors make judgements, based on evidence gathered from a variety of sources, about whether an individual meets a standard or a set of criteria. The idea of competency standards is essentially a development of criterion referenced assessment which evolved in North America, with the addition of a focus on the importance of assessment of performance, and its application particularly to vocational and professional education.

Competence cannot be observed directly, but it can be inferred from performance. Thus, we need to think about the sorts of performances which will enable us to gather evidence of sufficient quantity and quality to make sound judgements about an individual's competence. Such judgements cannot be absolute.

For large vocational education systems, an obvious problem with this approach is its practicability. For example, it may be harder to replicate more desirable assessment methods than, say, written tests, especially those based on recall of facts. And it is easier to demonstrate that the latter are "fair" or impartial—although, of course, they may not be valid! This is important where the credibility of qualifications has yet to be established, and decisions will often result from the need to balance external credibility against validity.

Recognition of Prior Learning

Recognition of Prior Learning (RPL), also called Accreditation of Prior Learning (APL) or Prior Learning Assessment (PLA), is a process to accredit learning gained or skills acquired outside formal educational institutions. A person might have learnt, for example, certain skills through voluntary community work, or through informal training within a company, or through non-credentialled courses. RPL emphasises what a person knows or can do, rather than how or when he or she learnt it. RPL is usually carried out by assessing what a person has learnt, or can do, against the standards required by the relevant course.

It is not, however, a procedure for giving credit for life experience.

Vocational education providers should take account of prior learning because it is sound educational practice: students may be able to progress more quickly, and they will not be forced to "learn" things they already know. The use of RPL for admission also has the potential to benefit women students', and those from disadvantaged socioeconomic backgrounds, who may be able to demonstrate ability even though they may lack formal qualifications.

There are financial benefits as well: both students and the nation may save money on unnecessary tuition, and the nation potentiary gains a member of the workforce more quickly. RPL have also served in some countries as a bridge between companies and vocational education providers, leading to more effective and better-recognised training. To carry out RPL successfully, it is necessary to clarify a number of issues about learning—both knowledge and skills—in order to identify the assessment principles which will guide successful practice.

The process of assessing a student's application entails a number of stages: preliminary information and advice, preparation of an application, assessment and accreditation, post-assessment guidance, and recording RPL results. It is also necessary to clarify exactly on what basis credit will be given, and to identify the most cost-effective way of conducting assessments in a particular subject area. That said, however, RPL may prove to be beneficial in a number of educational settings.

REFERENCES

Atkins, M. J., J. Beattie, and W. B. Dockrell, *Assessment issues in Higher education*, Sheffield, UK: Employment Department, 1993.

Boud, D., *Implementing student self-assessment*, (HERDSA Green no.5), 2nd edition, Sydney, Australia: Higher Education Research and Development Society of Australia, 1992

Eisner, E W., "Reshaping assessment in education: some criteria in search of practice", *Journal of Curriculum Studies 25* (3) 219-233., 1993.

Eckstein, M. A., and H. J. Noah, *Secondary School Examinations: International Perspectives on Policies and Practice*, Newhaven: Yale University Press, 1993.

Hagar, P., A. Gonczi, and Athanasou, J., "General issues about assessment of competence", *Assessment and Evaluation in Higher Educaiton* 19 (1) 3-16, 1994.

Rowtree, D., *Assessing students: how shall we know them*, (Second edition, revised), London: Kogan Page, 1989.

Simosko, S., *Accreditation of prior learning: a practical guide for professionals*, London: Kogan Page, 1991.

Wolf, A., *Competency-based assessment*, Milton Keynes, U.K.: Open University Press, 1994.

Whitaker, U., *Assessing learning: standards, principles and procedures*, Philadelphia: Council for Adult and Experimential Learning.

6

Challenges of Vocational Education

Vocational education and training policy is to offer people long-term employment opportunities through initial and continuing education and training. Young people must have real opportunities for gaining initial, solid vocational qualifications which open the door to skilled employment. People who do not yet possess any usable vocational qualifications should be offered various options for doing training at a later stage, which leads to officially recognised qualifications, thus enabling them to enter skilled employment. Furthermore, during their working lives, people must be given the chance to maintain and enhance their employability through lifelong learning, thus ensuring that the economy is provided with a sufficiently skilled workforce.

Today, employability is understood to be the acquisition of sound knowledge in a specialised field, along with skills and competences which enable an individual to exercise the occupation he or she has learned immediately after completing training. Vocational training is also expected to provide the basis for mobility within a profession and the employment market by teaching individuals the ability to achieve job success; furthermore it is expected to encourage willingness and foster the ability to engage in lifelong learning.

This ability and willingness must be maintained and further nurtured after the education and training period, which means that certain demands are placed on individuals and individual initiative. However, this notion must also be incorporated to a greater extent into the development strategies of companies and administrations. Consequently, increasing importance is being attached to improving the structures for lifelong learning, including in the workplace. More and more jobs require the ability to work independently, creativity, organisational skills and communication and cooperation skills.

A broad-based, vocational training course which is based on the needs of the employment system and offers initial job experience provides the necessary foundation. For this reason it is essential, from the point of view of both economic and social policy, that adequate numbers of training places are provided within the dual system of vocational training.

The dual system of vocational training, the vocational training institutions are being called upon to play an active role by ensuring that future generations of skilled employees are provided with modern and future-oriented training. In order to fulfil this educational task, the vocational training institutions must be equipped with the appropriate material and human resources.

Education and training policy, in particular vocational education and training policy, is being confronted by a series of deep-seated changes: industrialised nations are undergoing a fundamental structural transformation. They are now turning into global knowledge-information-and service-based economies. Due to the advance of information and communications technology, modern science and technology is permeating every area of life and work. This is not only bringing about changes in individual sectors of national economies and in international production and exchange relations.

At the same time, we are witnessing a fundamental demographic change whose impact on training and employment is still being underestimated. Low birth rates not only lead to decreasing population figures, but also, above all, to a different age structure of the population and thus of people of working age. The proportion of senior citizens is growing while the proportion of younger people and thus of the middle generation is decreasing. These two significant developments pose a huge challenge to the entire education system. The scenarios relating to the impact of the continued advance of modern information and telecommunications technologies in business and employment all centre on three linked trends:

i) The proportion of jobs involving actual production activities is diminishing while the proportion of jobs involving knowledge-based primary and, especially, secondary services is growing;
ii) The competent application of information and communications technologies is becoming a basic skill increasingly required for more and more jobs;
iii) International business and employment relations are intensifying and expanding, and this is affecting an increasing number of jobs.

As a result, the proportion of jobs demanding higher qualifications will rise sharply whereas the proportion of jobs demanding fewer qualifications will decrease. This will be accompanied at all levels of employment and at nearly all workplaces by rapid organisational and constant technological changes. This will give rise to new and continually changing requirements with regard to special and general skills.

In the future, the demand for skilled employees will also have to be satisfied by inviting qualified skilled employees from abroad. Thus one of the central tasks of education policy is to develop and exhaust employment and training potential over the next few years. Otherwise there is the risk that the problems arising from the mismatch between the education and training market and the employment market will increase. On the one hand, there is a shortage of jobs and training places in certain business sectors and regions, while, on the other hand, a certain number of jobs and training places are not being filled in other regions and future-oriented sectors.

To realise the principle of "vocational training for everyone", a large range of different training places must be provided in vocations which offer good job prospects on the employment market and are compatible with the different abilities and interests of young people. Responsibility lies first and foremost with the private sector.

The purpose of vocational training within the dual system is to open the door to skilled employment and to provide a solid basis for further vocational development. The rapid pace of changes in technology, processes and work procedures is forcing employees to continually adapt their qualifications and skills in order to remain employable in the long term. Thus it is necessary to make use of the various forms of continuing education, including learning in the workplace—an educational route that is becoming increasingly important.

For unskilled and semi-skilled employees, participation in continuing education will be made more attractive. Employers who grant unskilled or semi-skilled personnel leave to participate in training will be reimbursed the wages in full or in part. This is also intended to encourage employers to train unqualified employees.

Vocational training should, on the basis of a modern vocational concept, give people a foothold in a skilled occupation and at the same time lay the foundation for lifelong learning. A wide spectrum of diverse officially recognised occupations requiring formal training will cover the wide span of different interests and abilities among young people and also match the different qualification requirements of the employment market.

Vocational training is very important for creating equal opportunities for all young people. Qualified vocational training gives people a foothold in working life, which is increasingly characterised by rapidly changing qualification requirements in jobs and by a higher job fluctuation rate on the employment market.

In today's information and knowledge-based society everyone must expect to engage in continuing education and training throughout his or her working life. The consequence of this is that the rapid technological and organisational changes in the workplace will have to be successfully managed with an increasingly ageing workforce.

DEVELOPMENT OF TECHNICAL AND VOCATIONAL EDUCATION

Historically, technical and vocational education was seen as a way of preparing a workforce for industry. The new theory of economic development does not accept GDP as the prime indicator, because it can rise without enriching lives. The new approach argues that growth of income is essential—as means, not end—and states explicitly that development's primary objective is to benefit people, enhancing human capabilities to make a better life available to all. Thus the human development index, which measures well-being, is the indicator of development level, not GDP, which measures output.

Education enables a person to acquire skills. Training is the systematic preparation of individuals to improve their capacity to perform functions valued by the market and society. It imparts skills, so those functions can be performed better. It includes the full continuum of education, skill formation and training activities. Technical training emphasises background knowledge of the skills imparted and more skill-oriented, without creating much background knowledge.

Past economic development has produced rapid growth in some countries, but also rich/poor gulfs—many forms of inequality, and environmental deterioration. Depletion of natural capital, due to market failure to reflect full costs, cannot continue forever—so demands have risen for growth that is sustainable. This requires that, if one component of the total stock of capital is reduced, it must be replenished or offset by greater investment in another component. Increased potential output depends on increased capital (natural, physical, and human).

The new theory of development sees human capital as the prime engine of growth, with countries that have given priority to human capital formation performing well in growth, jobs, income equity and poverty alleviation. New technologies are making brain power the productive force, not muscle or machine power as before. Improved methods and more sophisticated products depend on customers and workers having sufficient information, training and education.

The universally recognised importance of investing in education—for economic growth and household welfare—is becoming even more crucial as the world economy grows more integrated. All countries must keep improving their workforce competence to face international competition and restructure their own economies.

For developing countries, skilled labour eases adoption of transferred technology and attracts investment. Technical and vocational education is a vital element in raising productivity and remaining competitive. Competitiveness has been defined as "the ability to produce goods and services that meet the test of international markets, while our citizens enjoy a standard of living that is both rising and sustainable," and as depending not on the fortunes of a country's companies or industries but on the functions performed by its workers within the global economy. Countries that open their economies and raise productivity by enhancing human capital can compete and eventually move into higher technology production.

Investing in education and training leads to high growth of income, productivity, investment and output, as well as faster technical progress, innovation, modernisation, and new capital goods. Such countries restructure industries efficiently and compete successfully on world markets. The effect is visible at plant level, where research shows dynamic firms providing much more training to far more workers than less dynamic firms. Educated, skilled labour also draws foreign investment.

Multinationals place units where workers have skills, or can acquire them—even for low-tech activities and certainly for higher-technology industries. Training provided by multinationals, locally or elsewhere, deepens a country's pool of workforce skills, increasing its capabilities. Thus foreign investment plus training sparks a 'virtuous circle' of development that helps a country use its resources for more advanced processes—increasing its competitiveness and encouraging restructuring of production and jobs, as technology changes and demand shifts.

Meanwhile, global competition is forcing developed countries to move away from traditional, labour-intensive 'sunset' industries (textiles, rubber, steel, autos), where imports are increasingly competitive, toward skill-intensive, high-tech 'sunrise' industries. Thus, to benefit from globalisation and technological change, a country must open its economy and move up to a higher level of technical capability, while ensuring the best use of resources—resulting in increased productivity, growth, and the export of more goods of higher technologies.

Technical and vocational education is vital to accelerated growth, and that workforce education is a significant determinant of productivity. In-house formal training raises productivity more than training from external sources, and training skilled workers is more effective than training unskilled workers.

South Asia failed to take full advantage of new global opportunities, because of infrastructure constraints such as widespread workforce illiteracy in India and Pakistan, where only a small percentage have any formal training. This means less efficient production, and a trend toward low-wage, low-skill employment in the informal sector, without access to training —which affects some industries and exports. India's leather industry employs 1.65 million people, 90 per cent in the informal sector, and her share of global exports has shrunk from lack of flexibility to adjust to new competition.

In software production, however, India—with skilled human resources and appropriate government support—has thrived: exports climbed roughly tenfold from 1987 to 1997.

India needs a national movement to enhance human capital, supported by government, industry, international organisations, and the public, in order to start a 'virtuous circle' of development.

Human capital investment is essential to a country's progress—but, alone, may not generate growth. Such outcomes could result if investment is poorly used or if the country pursues inappropriate development strategies. The right type of investment in human resources can take many forms—apprenticeship, on-the-job training, formal education, private study. It can be lifelong. It is an investment by employer and employee, with returns anticipated.

Productivity largely determines the standard of living. It is affected by many factors—investment, technical progress, government rules—but variation in education and training is the strongest determinant. However, the productivity gap between developed and developing countries has kept on growing, especially since the early 1980s, and may continue to increase rather than converge.

Development means profound change in the economy—a structural transformation that differs by country and time. The current, unprecedented global transformation challenges each society in various ways. Developing countries acquiring sunset industries and developed countries exploring high technology have different needs, and effective technical/vocational education must capture these swift changes and adjust quickly within a particular context, ideally with close cooperation between government, employers and workers.

In this information age, or post-industrial society, or mechatronic era, technical/vocational education must cope with the impact of microelectronics, computer-aided design (CAD) and manufacturing systems (CAMS), information technology, materials technology, and biotechnology, and an explosion of new industries.

Employment of skilled workers has risen worldwide in the 1980s and 1990s, particularly in the developed countries, where job growth has been mostly in the service sector and the information and communication technology industry, while administrative support staff and production workers have been displaced.

Demand for higher-skilled workers has grown less rapidly in the developing countries, and it has expanded in different directions. While structural transformation has opened doors for skilled workers, it has created instability, job loss, and risk of exclusion for large segments of the population. Globally, technical training and vocational education must:

i) reduce shortages of skilled workers,
ii) continuously upgrade workforce skill levels,
iii) respond to new forms of work organisation,
iv) help vulnerable groups escape unemployment,
v) adjust to service sector and microenterprise needs, and
vi) cope with the special situation of transition economies.

But each society has its own specific problems and needs. The one universal prerequisite for successful training is a foundational education—literacy and numeracy. Countries with a skilled workforce and growth-oriented policies are making progress, partly through investment in skill development, which helps increase employment. In other countries, with less ideal conditions, if unemployment exists partly because of a skills mismatch, training can clearly reduce joblessness. But if skills mismatch is not the problem, training would have little impact.

Persistent unemployment, which deepens poverty, is putting governments and training systems under pressure to help vulnerable groups avoid social exclusion and overcome systemic discrimination. Such groups—first fired, last hired, as economies fluctuate—cannot afford to upgrade their skills, have little access to education and credit, and are trapped in miserable marginalisation. In developed countries they compete for casual, temporary work; in developing countries, often with no social safety net, they rely on the insecure informal sector.

Training alone, without appropriate policies and social support, can do little to overcome the diverse obstacles to inclusion through employment: poor job growth; little access to education, training and credit; discrimination; government transfer policies that discourage work; rapid economic change; global competition; segmentation of the labour market; and, above all, lack of market-valued skill.

Low-skilled workers have few opportunities in manufacturing or even service industries. Training must be supported by micro-economic policies to improve access, and provide incentives to invest, as well as steps to encourage entrepreneurship and to counter discrimination. The informal sector—small firms, household enterprises, and self-employment—is huge and growing in developing countries. Based on easily acquired skills, it offers only low-wage jobs and little opportunity for upgrading.

Globalisation and structural change has opened some opportunities, but mainly in outsourcing, subcontracting, data processing and part-time work—mainly in low-wage, labour-intensive jobs where there is little incentive to invest in training. Women, more likely to spend time outside the labour force, need renewal and lifelong training but face restrictions on access to training schemes as well as traditional male domination of occupations and related training. Traditional welfare approaches are changing toward emphasis on equal treatment and rights—although many disabled workers in transition economies have lost once-guaranteed jobs.

Vocational rehabilitation services are sparse in the developing world. Technical and vocational education can improve productivity, make people employable, enhance human capital, attract investment, and ignite a 'virtuous circle' of development—if certain essential conditions exist. Otherwise, its role is very limited. Globalisation, competition, structural change in economies, new forms of work organisation, and many other social and economic factors are creating a new context for education and training.

CHANGING DEMAND

The role of vocational education in the context of the dynamics and changing demand of the world of work can better be explored through a more comprehensive approach to the overall system of human resources development (HRD). Human resources development, which is mainly implemented through the formal and non-formal systems of education, is the concern of both educationalists and economists. This is so because education is recognised both as a social service on the one hand, and an investment and hence economically feasible activity on the other. The existence of a link between education and economic development is mainly the result of human power needs being translated into educational targets and plans.

The relation between education and economic development is a complex one, because there exists no strict relationship between occupations and levels or types of education. Consequently, the ability and need to design manpower preparation and development systems based rigidly on the needs of employment requirements are questionable. The complexity of the relationship between education and economics is also due to the fact that education can be both a cause and an effect of economic development. This applies in particular to vocational education and training (VET), whose quality, size, standards, and diversification of offerings promote economic development on the one hand, and are strongly influenced by such development and work standards on the other.

Therefore, in manpower planning, which requires, among other things, the matching of supply and demand, such matching should emphasise interdependence, rather than dependence or independence, as a basic strategy. The criteria used for the evaluation of educational and HRD strategies and systems frequently reveal the differences in the views of economists and educationalists. Thus, the feasibility of a VET system can be assessed through the ability to secure employment, level of earnings, self and social image, job satisfaction, and the degree of lateral and upward mobility on the individual level; and through productivity levels, quality standards and national income figures on the national levels. To an educationalist, HRD, mainly through formal and non-formal education and training, should first be human and then professional, since such education and training should do more than provide the learner with the skills and knowledge specifically needed for his job, and since occupations are more effectively performed by individuals who are generally, as well as specifically prepared.

In the field of vocational and technical education individuals should be prepared to be intelligent users of the means of production rather than mere means of production. An economist, on the other hand, would emphasise the need for as accurate a matching of supply and demand in educational and manpower planning as possible, and would in general be sensitive to the 'marketability' of the 'products' of that educational system. Poorly balanced education systems, to an economist, are a waste of resources that are usually badly needed elsewhere.

Vocational and career guidance, from the point of view of economists, therefore, is oriented more to the fulfilment of market needs and the adjustment of learners' inclinations to such needs, than to the discovery of their abilities and inclinations and the realisation of their potentials and educationally justified ambitions. Planners are in general frequently faced with the dilemma of whether to sacrifice some of the individual aspirations and social ideals to ensure the adequacy of manpower supply, or to sacrifice the fulfilment of some of the economic needs to better respond to individual claims and social pressures.

Every occupation comprises a great number of functions, tasks and skills performed by individuals of varying performance, ability and degree of responsibility, thus requiring different occupational and skill levels as part of the more comprehensive 'division of labour' concept. In practice the skill ladder is usually divided into 'bands' to simplify the process of classification, the hierarchy of responsibility, and the design of human power development programmes.

Occupational levels at the top of the skill ladder include professionals and technicians (sub-professionals) who are usually prepared in tertiary level educational institutions; while occupational levels at the base of the skill ladder comprise skilled workers and craftsmen prepared frequently within secondary education or parallel to it. A professional or specialist is in general, prepared in institutes of university level. A sub-professional or technician, on the other hand, is prepared usually in educational institutes of sub-university, but within the tertiary, level of education such as community and technical colleges. The basic occupational levels, which comprise various categories of craftsmen, skilled workers and limited-skills workers, are not usually defined internationally in terms of the required educational levels as is the case with upper occupational levels of professionals and technicians.

Different countries have different standards, educational backgrounds and systems of manpower preparation at the basic occupational levels, although it is becoming more and morc accepted that such levels lie at least within the senior stage of secondary education or parallel to it, inside or outside the formal education system. Occupational classifications and standards within the various occupational levels is an area that has important reflections on both the development and utilisation aspects of human power. Employers should be full partners in the initialisation, development and implementation of the relevant activities. Apart from the fact that such classifications and standards should emanate from the changing demand of the world of work, they have direct influence on such matters as wage structures, labour mobility and performance standards of the labour force. A big deficit or surplus at the higher occupational levels can be as much a source of imbalance and economic weakens as a similar deficit or surplus at the basic occupational levels. Three main systems exist in practice for VET as a component of HRD frameworks and institutions. One or more of such systems might exist in any one country.

These systems are:

a) *The school system:* The school system for VET is usually implemented in formal educational institutions. The trainee, who is thus a student in a vocational school or training centre, acquires his vocational preparation through some approved formal programmes in the educational institution itself., with little or no direct contact with the world of work. The relevant programmes consist usually of general and specialised theoretical components, in addition to the practical component which is implemented almost exclusively in special workshops and laboratories attached to the school. Nevertheless, it is not unusual for a school system to develop some useful links with the world of work. Such links could incorporate training standards, and an element of on-the-job training.

b) *The enterprise (on-the-job) system:* The enterprise system is implemented on-the-job at the workplace and employers premises. The trainee, who is thus either a full-fledged worker or under special contract, acquires his vocational preparation on-the-job, with emphasis being placed on the practical skills component. Enterprise systems vary between informal traditional apprenticeship schemes on one end, and well-structured apprenticeship schemes on the other end.

c) *The integrated (dual) system:* The integrated or dual system for VET combines both the school and the enterprise systems. The implementation takes place partially in educational institutions and partially in enterprises, with full coordination. The role of the educational institution comprises usually the theoretical instruction component which might include a general education element in addition to the specialised element. In some schemes, the educational institution provides some elements of the practical skills needed, especially basic non-specialised and back-up skills that cannot be provided by the relevant enterprise. The role of the

> enterprise, on the other hand, comprises basically all or most of the practical training component, especially for the specialised parts of it. The involvement of employers within the dual system could incorporate, in addition to the provision of training facilities, the appointment of full or part-time instructors; and the payment of apprenticeship wages to the trainees.

The training programme, including the detailed contents and certification is usually drawn up through full coordination between the concerned parties, although the relevant training standards are expected to be drawn up by the enterprise. Formal apprenticeship schemes with a substantial off-the-job element is the usual model for dual systems. In such systems, the trainee is, in practice, a worker under training and a student in an educational institution at the same time. In the case of large enterprises, the off-the-job educational facilities can be provided at the employers' premises. The question of whether vocational preparation should be the responsibility of the education system or that of the enterprise is a major issue, especially in developing countries.

If vocational, and hence manpower, preparation is interpreted broadly to comprise any type and level of education and training made available to the individual to prepare him for his future vocation, then most, if not all, of higher education at the professional and sub-professional levels in universities and technician institutes can be classified as vocational preparation. But at these higher occupational levels, the predominant responsibility of the education system is taken for granted; although, in some countries, technician education in particular is a shared responsibility. Therefore, it is vocational education and training for the preparation of skilled workers and craftsmen at the basic occupational levels that is contested in practice between the school and the enterprise.

Those who support a school-based model of manpower preparation at the basic occupational levels require that the education system should be responsible for the policy making, planning and overall content specification and criteria. The rationale for such an approach stems from the view that education is an activity intended for the development of the individual and, thus, encompasses both general and vocational education. Such a view assumes that the enterprise is unable to take overall responsibility for manpower preparation without running the risk that one-sided narrow economic criteria will govern the various aspects of the training programme, including its objectives, content, standards and quality.

The supporters of an enterprise-based model of manpower preparation at the basic occupational levels believe that, because such preparation is mainly connected with the requirements of the enterprise, it should have little place in school. The scope of responsibilities of the enterprise in this case includes policy making, planning, standards setting and content specification. Industry-based vocational preparation schemes are, in general, more economical than school-based ones. This is because productive work can more readily be undertaken by trainees, and because of the possibility of utilising existing facilities, at least partially, instead of establishing new ones. But a major consideration in this respect is the fact that the greater part of the training cost is usually distributed among employers. It is usually argued in support of the enterprise approach that, at the basic occupational levels, the training needs of industry can more effectively be responded to through in-plant training because of its relevance, flexibility, cost effectiveness and ability to offer smooth transition to work. In practice, the school system is often at a disadvantage when new specific training needs emerge, and frequently runs the risk of a mismatch between its output and employment requirements.

In many countries, two separate systems of vocational preparation at the basic occupational levels exist side by side: one is school based and the other is enterprise based. This can partially be attributed in developing countries to the fact that industrial development is rather new and partial. Formal in-plant vocational preparation is thus a newcomer, while a traditional school-based system would have been in existence for some time. The introduction of the in-plant system is usually facilitated by the expanding needs of the new industrial developments and the inability of the education system to respond effectively both quantitatively and qualitatively.

Evaluation of Vocational Education

Three main criteria exist for the evaluation of VET programmes. As will be seen, such criteria are linked with varying degrees to the criteria and changing demands of the world of work:

i) *Internal evaluation:* The internal evaluation of VET programmes is generally concerned with assessing the degree of compatibility between the outputs of such programmes and the performance objectives already set out for them. Such evaluation can be implemented through various measures, including the assessment of:

   a) trainee performance and achievement.
   b) trainer proficiency and performance.
   c) training programme.
   d) training facilities.

Internal evaluation has an indirect link with the world of work, and can be isolated from it. Nevertheless, such a link can be strengthened through the involvement of employers in the assessment of the various elements covered by internal evaluation.

2) *Economic evaluation:* The economic evaluation of VET programmes can be considered part of the internal evaluation of such programmes. It is concerned mainly with the assessment of such indicators as:

   i) efficiency of utilisation of training facilities.
   ii) cost-benefit rates.
   iii) lost income by the trainee during the training period.

iv) extra income gained by the trainee, that is attributed to the training programme.

v) comparative studies related to the cost of different VET systems.

vi) the rise in productivity at the workplace, that can be attributed to the training programme.

As in the case of internal evaluation, most elements of the economic evaluation of VT programmes have an indirect link with the world of work, although an element like the influence of VET programmes on productivity has a direct link with the workplace.

3) *External evaluation:* Unlike the internal and economic kinds of evaluation which are inherently inward looking, the external evaluation of VET programmes is outward looking, as it is basically concerned with assessing the degree of compatibility between the relevant programme, including its performance, objectives and outputs, on the one hand, and employment requirements and work needs on the other. External evaluation is especially important in the case of school systems which usually run the risk of losing contact with the world of work. It can be implemented through various measures, including the assessment of:

   i) results of follow-up studies on graduates.

   ii) employment-unemployment characteristics of graduates.

   iii) the time lag, if any, between the completion of training and joining employment.

   iv) wage structures.

   v) adaptation time needed to assume full production status.

   vi) the size and type of special and initiation training that should be provided by the employer.

vii) feedback information from the employers.
viii) feedback information from employed graduates.
ix) productivity and work standards.

It is very clear that a direct link exists between the external evaluation of VET programmes and the world of work. In fact, such evaluation is rooted in the needs and requirements of the world of work. It is worth noting that a comprehensive assessment of VET programmes takes into consideration all three kinds of evaluation, especially that a positive outcome of one kind does not necessarily indicate that a similar outcome can be expected from the other two kinds.

The role of the world of work, represented by the various types of enterprises in vocational education and training, can be explored through four main functions: planning, financing, implementation, and identification of training needs. The following is a brief discussion of each of these functions.

The quality and efficiency of VET systems depend, to a great extent, on the quality of planning for such systems. The credibility and effectiveness of the planning function, on the other hand, is closely related to the involvement of all the concerned agencies, not the least of which are the employers whose enterprises are the main target for VET programmes. The involvement of the private sector in the planning function for VET can assume many forms, and can be realised through different measures. These include:

a) *Legislation:* Laws, by-laws and regulations in such fields as labour, employment, education and human resources development, can be utilised to provide the legislative umbrella and legal framework for defining the role of the world of work in the planning for HRD in general, and for VET in particular.

b) *Institutional frameworks:* The involvement of the private sector in the institutional setups related to the planning for VET can be secured through active and full-fledged participation of employers' representatives in the relevant boards, councils, commissions and committees responsible for the planning and supervision functions at the institution and local levels, as well as on the systems and national levels.

c) *Curriculum development:* Employers' participation in curriculum development for VET systems and programmes is an important aspect of the private sector involvement in the planning function. Through such participation, the employment and labour market needs of the various VET programmes can rationally be taken into consideration.

d) *Information systems:* The availability of effective information systems is essential for the provision of the necessary database needed for planning activities. Information systems in this case should cover both the supply and the demand sides of human power. The quantitative and qualitative aspects of human power and training needs of the various economic sectors are the major components in such database, which can be secured through full coordination and cooperation between the word of work and the relevant public and private sector agencies.

Practices vary considerably between countries as to the sources and means of funding for VET systems and programmes. In general, VET can be funded through four main sources:

a) *Taxpayers*: Funding from the taxpayers through the state budget is an option which is sometimes resorted to when VET is viewed as a national responsibility which should be shouldered by the whole population according to the income level of the various cohorts. This source of funding is common in many countries, especially in developing countries; and is usually utilised to finance school systems of VET. It has the disadvantage of sometimes being inadequate, especially in countries with limited resources, because it is not given due priority in national budgets.

b) *Employers:* Funding of VET from industry and business in the private sector is an option that gains credibility when VET is viewed as an activity earmarked for the direct benefit of the employers. Apprenticeship schemes, on-the-job training, and dual systems of training are examples of VET schemes that are usually funded, totally or partially, by employers, in addition to paying the wages of instructors and training officers. In some cases, a special tax or training levy is applied on industrial and business enterprises to secure funding for national VET systems.

c) *Beneficiaries:* According to this funding option, the learners, trainees and their families, who are considered the main beneficiaries of the relevant VET services on the individual level, are expected to meet the costs, totally or partially. Training fees, acceptance of reduced wages, and involvement in productive activities, are some of the practices that lead to the involvement of trainees in the funding of VET. When VET is utilised for the preparation and training of skilled workers and craftsmen at the basic occupational levels, charging training fees is not common practice, except when private (profit or non-profit making) institutions and agencies are the providers of the relevant services.

d) *Voluntary efforts:* Donations, grants and fund-raising activities can be an important source of funding for VET services, especially when such services are targeted to special groups of the population, including the handicapped and the underprivileged.

The role of the world of work in the implementation of VET programmes can be categorised into two main groups of activities. The first group is generally related to in-service training activities for those who are already employed. Such activities are usually of short-duration nature and include such variations as initiation training for the newly appointed employees, re-training for new jobs and skills, and upgrading training to raise the competence of employees and enhance their productivity. The second group is related to pre-service education and training activities, such as formal and non-formal types of apprenticeship, aiming at the full preparation of labour for the needs of the enterprise through a programme of vocational education and training which, in this case, is usually of longer duration and a more comprehensive nature.

The positive role of the enterprise in the first category of in-service training activities for employees at all occupational levels has long been taken for granted, and employers are realising more and more how important it is to have a comprehensive policy for the development of the skills and abilities of their workforce. The services and facilities needed for such in-service training activities can be provided either "in-house" by the enterprise itself, or by an external agency. It is in the field of the second category of pre-service vocational preparation programmes, to prepare skilled workers and craftsman, that practices and judgements differ considerably, as shown earlier.

REFERENCES

Dempsey, R., "Resource Document, Occupational Information for the Skill Standards Projects", 1994.

Grubb, W.N, & C. Stasz, *Assessing the integration of academic and vocational education: Methods and questions*, University of California, Berkeley,1992.

Little, J. W., *Two Worlds: Vocational and Academic Teachers in Comprehensive High Schools*, 1992.

Oakes, J., M. Selvin, L, Karoly, G, Guiton, *Educational Matchmaking: Academic and Vocational Tracking in Comprehensive High Schools*, 1992.

Plihal, J., M.A. Johnson, C. Bentley, C. Morgaine, T. Liang, *Integration of Vocational and Academic Education: Theory and Practice*, 1992.

Wills J.L., E. Rice, and R. Sheets, "An Overview of Skill Standards Systems in Education and Industry", *Systems in the U.S. and Abroad*, Volume IV, 1993.

7

Vocational Education and Training

In almost all the countries in the world education is provided in both the public and the private sectors. A certain minimum level of education is necessary for a country to achieve economic growth. The allocation of resources to education varies in each country in accordance with its priorities but generally ranges from 3 to 8 per cent of the gross national product.

The overall costs on education are on the increase. Developing countries are particularly hard hit due to the economic crisis. They need to improve productivity to enable them to compete in an era of rapid economic and technological change. This requires both capital investment and a workforce with the flexibility for acquiring new skills for new jobs. They are also faced with the challenge of meeting the requirements of the education sector, to fulfil the overall responsibility vested in the state for development of human resources.

Governments cannot shift this responsibility as education confers benefits to the society at large. It can at best harness the support of the private sector, the community and individuals in its endeavour to reach its goals towards social and economic development of the country. While budgetary constraints are prevailing everywhere it is more severe in countries which have completely public financed education systems.

Some of the reasons for the crisis in financing education are increase in demand for access to education, increase in teachers' salaries, inefficiency in the use of available resources, demographic growth creating additional demand for schooling facilities, unemployment of graduates, increase in the costs of land and buildings, etc. Reform in financing has to come about by modifying financing modes. Some ways could be that users should bear some part of the costs as entire public funding cannot be justified; there should be more efficient management of funds, search for private financing, community and enterprise involvement, and foreign aid.

As budget allocations from government sources for education get tighter, the squeeze on availability of funds for Vocational Education and Training (VET) is apparent in so far as VET is dependent on public funds. Costs on VET as compared with general education are also two to three times higher as classes are small with instructor trainee ratios of 1:7 sometimes. This increases the unit teaching costs. Expenditure on equipment, infrastructure, consumables, e.g., raw materials and spare parts, is also much higher. It is then imperative to search for alternative means of financing.

The challenge before policy makers is to introduce new and different ways of financing as well as to ensure that the resources which are available for VET are used more effectively. Traditionally, VET was provided by employers who paid lower wages and sometimes apprentices had to pay the employer. This was prevalent in many different countries.

In Germany, approximately since the twelfth century, a person was allowed to pursue a trade independently if he had finished the apprenticeship in a craft with a master. After apprenticeship he had to obtain professional experience as a journeyman. The master taught his apprentice and journeyman the knowledge of his trade. The craftsmen got united and formed guilds and evolved a proper training system. The main responsibility for vocational training lay with the craftsmen's organisations and all conditions were regulated by the guild. Traditional apprenticeship also existed in India for centuries.

Even today in towns and villages it is a very common sight to observe an apprentice working with the master, learning by working on the job, all at a very early age. In the former times in India apprentices often lived with the master and there was a certain unity in living, learning and working. In the small by- lanes of towns and cities in countries like Indonesia, Nepal, Bangladesh and India it is very common to see young apprentices in the age group of 10-20 years being trained by their employers, e.g., the bicycle repair, the auto mechanics workshop. They go straight 'on the job'. Sometimes in the initial stages there is no payment. As they learn the work they begin to get a small wage.

The costs are shared by the employer who provides the training and the worker who accepts low wages. In the modern times the scenario has somewhat changed. Gradually governments have become more involved in VET, especially in the last two decades. This is mainly to link vocational education and training with the social, economic and employment policies of the country.

Public revenue for VET has assumed more importance. But owing to the economic crisis governments had to reduce the public budgets for education, and this has a direct bearing on all sectors of education including VET. Serious attempts have to be made to find resources to supplement available funds. Every country has to assess its training needs and requirements in accordance with its goals and priorities and the prevailing socio-economic conditions. Thereafter strategies for financing VET have to be worked out and additional resources generated. While governments are searching for new and alternative mechanisms, the private sector is being drawn in justifiably, for those who benefit must pay for it.

The relevance of vocational education to the labour market requirements is crucial. As the employers become more involved in the actual provision of vocational education and training it will come closer to labour market needs influenced particularly by the rapid technological change.

Vocational Training Institutes (VET) are set up with new and modern training methods being offered. This has naturally led to questions being raised about the costs of training and the mechanisms of financing it. It is difficult to estimate the exact costs on VET due to the complexities involved in the training systems, the absence of accurate accounts by employers, and the productive work of the apprentices/trainees who accept lower wages and thereby offset part of the costs incurred. Nevertheless, studies have concentrated on the total amount of funds allocated for VET and its adequacy.

Governments are therefore getting more concerned about financing of vocational training to meet the new and emerging labour market requirements. Various financing strategies are practised in different parts of the world. Some of the more well known mechanisms for financing VET have been categorised in the following four types:

i) Public Financing
ii) Enterprise Financing
iii) Private and Public Sponsored Financing
iv) International Donor Assistance.

PUBLIC FINANCING

Traditionally vocational training was provided by employers who paid lower wages or no wages at all to the trainees. Employers did this if it increased productivity of workers. In many cases, the government was only involved with standards of training. Involvement of governments increased mainly to link vocational education and training more closely with social, economic and employment policies of the country. There was also a growing concern about distribution of training opportunities for the poorer and disadvantaged sections of the society. Public Financing is provided through public revenue.

When the state finances vocational training through public funds it is on the assumption that the ultimate responsibility for development of human resources for national development lies with the state. Governments also intervene in the provision of vocational training to ensure social equity for the poor in the rural and urban informal sector. Public financed VET provides opportunities to persons who may otherwise have limited chances, e.g., those from the deprived sections of the society.

Public financed vocational training programmes are implemented in schools before employment is taken up. Non-formal training centres, pre-service and in-service training for ministries also receive public funding. Specialised vocational training institutions receive public funds mainly through subsidies, budget appropriations, tax incentives, financing of special programmes with special grants, financing of development projects, financing of supervisory bodies, and fellowships for VET.

In developing countries, e.g., Pakistan, India and Thailand the main financial contribution for VET comes from public funds (government). Industry takes little part in contributing to vocational training institutes. In cases of mixed funding, generally capital expenditurc is provided by the governments and recurring expenditure is shared through other sources. Public vocational training institutions generally offer courses which provide basic skills necessary in pre-service training.

In many countries owing to a shortage of skilled manpower governments had to create proper vocational training systems for long term social returns of training, need for equal opportunities of training for those who are unable to pay costs of their training, and to promote national VET policies. The cost effectiveness of vocational training through public financing is said to be low as public training institutions are not very keen to evaluate the qualitative and quantitative training needs. When public training institutions are expanded and do not get adequate finances correspondingly the quality of training may become poor.

Open unemployment among graduates exceeds 35 per cent. In Bangladesh and Cameroon less than half of public trainees find wage employment in their trade. Public training has to respond to the demand in the labour market, only then can it become cost effective with good quality training leading to high placement rates. Public contributions are controlled by restrictive policies.

Vocational training institutions which are dependent solely on public funds have the chance of becoming stagnant with a deterioration in their planning and efficiency. Sometimes subsidies to vocational training institutions are dependent on the goodwill of the government.

The advantages of public financing are:

i) When government finances vocational training through public revenue it can coordinate the requirements in accordance with the demand projected in the economic and employment policies.

ii) Matching grants encourage local initiative as institutions wishing to receive grants from the government try to raise resources on their own.

iii) Categorial aid usually helps to implement change as it is given for a specific purpose or to meet the needs of specific target groups in the population.

iv) Through both these methods of financing, governments can share control and at the same time have part of the financial burden shared by others.

v) In the initial stages, national training centres are said to develop better in centralised systems as the institutional capacities are not strong. But centralisation is not desirable when institutions become well developed. At that stage more autonomy is required.

vi) In public distribution systems there is more equity. Publicly financed vocational training systems offer opportunities to the poorer sections of the society. For them it may be the only opportunity to become trained.

ENTERPRISE FINANCING

The enterprise/company conducts the vocational training of its labour force directly and bears the entire costs of training. Often enterprises finance a major part of the training but actual training occurs in specialised vocational training institutions. Sometimes enterprises contribute a small amount of money to a central vocational training fund as taxes, and these resources are used in different ways to finance training.

In many countries where employers are active participants in VET a Training Fund for financing vocational training has been set up. Tax contributions from the employers collected through payroll levies or subsidies from the government are transferred to the Training Fund. Every firm gets a drawing right which is a fraction of its contribution. The remaining amount is mutualised. Every firm retains a certain degree of autonomy and the Fund also has some reserves.

The advantages of enterprise financing are:

i) When individual companies train their own work force, such as in Japan, they can tailor their requirements in accordance with the actual needs. This leads to effective management policies and avoids wastage of trained manpower.

ii) When training occurs alongside production it reduces the overall costs on training.

iii) Training and employment in one company or enterprise gives stability to the individual and to the company.

iv) A study of financing of vocational training in Latin America indicated that payroll taxes proved to be an effective financing mechanism as it helped to create training institutions that are workable and good alternatives to traditional training systems.

v) Payroll levies are found to be more successful in middle income countries. They are effective in addressing the training needs of large formal sector enterprises. Also effective in strengthening government, employers and labour cooperation.

vi) Payroll levies are shouldered by enterprises but part of the costs fall on workers in the form of lower wages. This leads to sharing of costs as workers subsidise their own training.

vii) Although training costs are high for the national training agencies yet quality of training programmes is better and linked to employers needs.

viii) Larger enterprises benefit more through tax rebates and credits. In 1985, in Singapore all the firms with 200 or more employees applied for training grants in contrast to 25 per cent of firms with 50 employees or less. Firms which had 10 employees or less only 2.2 per cent applied for grants.

ix) Tax credits are more effective in matured or maturing economies.

x) When seen from a broader perspective VTI's compete with each other to train manpower required by the enterprises. This encourages efficiency within the institutions.

xi) As the Vocational Training Fund observes the labour market closely and has regular interaction with business and industrial houses, it can influence the organisation of appropriate VET programmes in accordance with labour market demand.

xii) It can also influence the quality of training. As it negotiates funding of training with business and industrial houses, to an extent it effectively regulates industrial relations.

xiii) Through the process of mutualisation the Fund can provide resources for training to small firms and enterprises which may not otherwise have enough access to training. As such it can offer equal training opportunities to firms.

The Training Fund is an important mechanism of financing VET and can diversify its funding, depending on the quality of financial services it offers.

PRIVATE AND PUBLIC SPONSORED FINANCING

Governments faced with a shortage of resources would like individuals, enterprises and non-government organisations (NGOs) to share the financial responsibility for VET. In some cases the entire operational costs are borne by the participants through payment of fees. More commonly, employers or trainees bear part of the costs and government finances the remaining. Fees could be paid to the government or the training institution.

Money raising through productive work is widespread in primary and secondary schools. In vocational training programmes, while students learn they also produce. But a high percentage of costs cannot be offset through productive activities. Generally the most effective programmes are operated by NGOs which have greater flexibility. One would assume that the product which is best for the training institution to sell is training itself.

Advantages of private and public sponsored financing:

i) Training fees enhance efficiency and contribute resources as well. Participants are likely to pay for training if it is of good quality and can bring personal benefits and high private rates of return.

ii) Fee level can control excessive demand as fees can be raised if there is more demand.

iii) If fees are high the quality may improve.

iv) Fees are found to be effective in financing short term training in the informal sector. Master craftsmen are paid small stipends for additional training which they give in approved sites.

v) Loans are good for financing short term training.

vi) Sale of training services facilitate additional income for Vocational Training Institutes.

vii) Co-financing agreements raise the resource level of VTI's.

viii) Training can be organised in accordance with demand and therefore enhance training-employment linkages.

ix) Dual training system is beneficial to firms although cost figures are difficult to calculate due to hidden expenditures, e.g., breakage and waste of materials, lower productivity of experienced workers who spend time in instructing apprentices. Work of apprentices also offsets costs.

x) Dual system is an efficient system of financing by individual firms, and it is doubtful if better results could be achieved in Germany with another financing system. From 1980 to 1984 the number of college graduates entering the dual system rose from 20,000 to 80,000.

xi) Production for profit can offset a small percentage of costs. In low income countries school production may help to supply goods and services when there are shortages.

xii) Paid educational leave motivates the workers/ employees to upgrade their skill levels. Higher and more skills contribute to productivity.

xiii) NGOs generally work for charitable causes contributing to the socio-economic development of the country. When they become involved in vocational training they take over the liability of financing some of the costs which would otherwise fall on the government.

xiv) As they are highly motivated and often work for the upliftment of the poorer and weaker sections of the society, their contribution leads to social equity.

xv) They are mostly very successful in providing short term training.

xvi) NGOs operating in the rural and urban informal sectors generally have a good knowledge of the local market. Thus they can effectively link training with the local employment requirement.

xvii) Non-profit making NGOs generally have dedicated persons on their management. They are keenly engaged in offering good quality vocational training and can thus provide effective support to vocational training systems.

INTERNATIONAL DONOR ASSISTANCE

Donor support plays a very important role in developing VET systems. In many developing countries the large amount of international aid has contributed to the setting up of a base of training capacity. Infrastructure and facilities have been created, staff trained and instructional systems implemented through donor assistance.

Mostly donors provide financial resources for capital costs and it is limited for short periods. In the 1980s, international assistance to vocational and technical education and training averaged about $ 600 million annually of which the World Bank provided 45 per cent, bilateral agencies 30 per cent and other multilateral agencies 25 per cent. Approximately 40 per cent of multilateral assistance for education was used to support VET programmes.

From 1963 to 1976, 40 per cent of lending for education by the World Bank was for VET at the secondary and post-secondary levels. But evaluations conducted in the 1970's regarding cost effectiveness of vocational schooling especially diversified schools began to raise doubts.

The advantages are:

i) Donor assistance helps to set up vocational training institutions.

ii) In some of the low income countries, but for donor support, it may not be possible to create infrastructure required for VET.

iii) Donor assistance facilitates transfer of latest productive technology to low income countries which can stimulate economic growth.

iv) Donors provide technical assistance from countries which have been successful in vocational training.

Governments will continue to finance VET through public revenue as the overall responsibility for development of human resources in the country rests with it. Without adequate investment in education, it is almost impossible to promote development. Government support in financing VET will therefore continue to flow and remain the most reliable. With diversification of financing mechanisms, however, larger resources are available for creating more training opportunities.

But the problems of financing VET cannot be solved entirely through diversification of resources. Efforts have to be made to better utilise available resources by removing existing inefficiencies, stricter accountability, improving organisational structures and proper application of new information technology. Vocational training systems should remain flexible with the ability to adapt to the changing social, economic and technological requirements of the country.

Vocational training systems should continue its search for generating additional resources through the public and private sectors such as government subsidies, enrolment fees in the long term or contributions from associations and unions. They should maintain a certain proportion of income from payroll levies and use it effectively for encouraging co-financing with enterprises. They could include decentralised and local bodies in the sale of general services to adapt to the new requirements of the governments. They should also make use of non-monetary contributions in the form of equipment and new materials for the training centres which may be donated through agreements with business. If vocational training systems are very large and programme activities cannot be adequately supported, it may be better to reduce the programmes and consolidate the existing resources and reallocate them appropriately.

The important thing is effective management of the institution through a proper balance between capital and recurrent expenditures. All training components should be strengthened and emphasis should be on quality training. The management should work closely with the employers. Diversification of resources is not easily possible in countries which have highly centralised systems with rigid controls. New ways of raising resources will require new working relationships with religious bodies and trade associations, and that requires delegation of authority.

The economic situation in the country also affects the financing mechanism. In low income countries there is a shortage of resources in the government. At the same time it is not possible to find many suitable alternatives to government funding. In the middle income countries there are greater possibilities for diversifying financing, and experience has shown that it is possible to have different forms of vocational education and training. Strategies for financing VET have to take into account the pattern of economic development. There is no optimal combination of financing.

In most countries there is a need to diversify training, and new ways of financing may lead to new ways of training. Attempts to diversify financing will ensure stability in the long term as it will reduce excessive dependence on a single source. There is no single or universal solution for financing vocational training and no one method which can serve all sections of the society. There are many different limitations in every system. Questions about who should meet the costs, the employers, individuals or the government are raised from time to time.

REFERENCES

Caillods, F., "Converging trends amidst diversity vocational training systems", *International Labour Review,* Vol. 133, no. 2, Geneva, ILO, 1994.

Carnoy, M., "Efficiency and equity in vocational education and training policies", *International Labour Review, Vol. 133*, no.2, Geneva, ILO, 1994.

Cinterfor, ILO, "Vocational training on the threshold of the 1990s", *PHREE Background Paper Series, Document No. PHREE/91/35*, Washington, D.C.: World Bank, 1991.

De Moura, Castro, C., "Training policies for the end of the century", *New trends in technical and vocational education*, Paris: UNESCO/IIEP, 1995.

Dougherty, C., J. P. Tan, "Financing training, issues and options", *PRE Working paper series, WPS716*, Washington D.C.: World Bank, 1991.

8

Technologies and Training in TVE

The reasons for using New Technologies and Training (NTTs) in Education and Training are multiple. They may help in improving the quality of the teaching/learning process, reducing training time and costs, complementing the lack of education opportunities in certain places at certain times. Improving quality is probably the most important reason. The introduction of NTTs increases learning attractiveness and therefore its effectiveness. Tests have demonstrated that an improved quality of training material and media increases the retention rate by 30 to 40 per cent, which is not negligible. This may be due to different factors, such as better adaptation to the individual learning styles.

Increased retention may reduce failure rates and consequently training length and costs. For young people, used to playing with technology outside the school, the use of NTTs in education creates or maintains motivation to learn; it also indicates the necessity that schools should not remain behind the rest of the world but should keep abreast with it, and prepare learners to use technology in their working life. Another aspect is the opportunity offered by NTTs to provide certain learners with the prerequisites required to enter a course of study; the teacher then has a more homogeneous class, which works faster and better. Quality may also result from the simulation of reality, where complexity, cost and for danger would make it difficult to undertake training in real-life conditions. Typical examples are simulating econometric models of the economy, aircraft flight simulators, chemical experiences with explosive products, etc.

The importance of simulation in education and training is growing. It allows the leaner to test several sets of parameters, and to create various environments whose effects can be computed and studied until the optimal solution is found. Quality training may considerably reduce the dropout rate. Increased quality of training media motivates learners who generally accomplish their training up to the end, which is not, always the case, for example, in distance-learning courses using only printed materials.

TRAINING ENVIRONMENT

Once the decision has been taken to implement NTTs, it is essential to be sure that those who will have to use them, teachers and learners, are convinced that NTTs will improve their teaching or learning process. If this is not the case, it is worthless to invest time and money in them because the equipment would be under-utilised. This process generally takes some time and is done step by step:

a) If it is decided to develop the titles oneself, one has to decide which hardware (computer and audiovisual) and software (authoring and/or presentation systems, graphics tools) has to be ordered. Ordering, receiving and installing hardware and software, not to speak about training those who will have to use them, usually takes longer than is generally expected; hence the necessity to do it as soon as possible in the overall process.

b) If the institution has decided to develop titles itself, the next step generally consists of organising hands-on workshops for those who will develop; it is indeed different to watch something done by somebody else (demonstrations) from being allowed to actually practices;

which generally suppresses a great deal of fear towards the difficulty of using NTTs.

c) Most trainers/teachers and courseware developers probably do not know NTTs, or at least those NTTs which will be used. Their training for a good utilisation is essential to the success of the whole operation. Again, this is by not means a waste of time but a good investment in staff development.

d) Prototype courses, or modules, will then be developed and tested on a representative sample of learners. This will help answer those questions the teachers and developers are asking themselves, and allow them to check whether the learners' reactions are what they thought they would be. Lessons gained from this test will be more than useful in the development of courses.

e) Usually developed titles are performed by a multi disciplinary team. People who are not used to working together will have to learn to do so! Graphic artists, computer specialists, subject matter experts, etc., are indeed not used to speaking to each other, and have very different points of view, which may enhance their interest in a common undertaking.

Trends

Some trends about new technologies and education for the next few years are already visible in the most recent hardware and software announcements, research and experimental applications, educational titles offerings, and debates in international conferences. Some of the trends mentioned below are already being implemented on a restricted basis, as prototypes or experiments; it is wise to consider them as trends for as long as they are not generalised.

NTTs will be more and more powerful (faster microprocessors, faster and bigger memories, faster and larger storage systems, better display quality, faster and more complex printers, etc.). The same applies to software: easier to use, more functions, etc.

Standardisation will improve, in all domains: audio and video files, compression techniques, file formats, etc., which means faster and cheaper development of additional learning material, easier translation into other languages, easier adaptation to other cultures, etc.

The move from analogue to digital will continue and probably go as far as possible. This will increase the possibility to exchange learning material, to send it via computer networks, to store it in computer databases, etc. It also allows the use of compression techniques.

The teachers' role will undergo a change from what it is today, it will be seen more as that of a guide, a counsellor who helps learners to discover, understand the subject matter, delivered by NTTs. This supposes a considerably different approach to teachers' training and retraining, and, even more important, acceptance of the new role by the teachers themselves.

This is probably a critical challenge for the 1990's. Some people say that teachers should become chameleons to adapt themselves to NTTs. Retraining of teachers already at work might have to be done on the job with the support of NTTs. Leaners will of course have to change their way of learning from a rather passive mode to a very active one, helped by teachers and tutors in their new roles, and by NTTs.

Teachers and learners will have to be part of a multimedia literate educational community, in order to get the most from the use of NTTs. All this will be possible, or at least easier, thanks to the implementation of networked multimedia, also called multimedia distributed, computing: as a first step, multimedia capabilities are extended from stand-alone PCs to the whole range of products (workstations, minicomputers, mainframes) allowing the same software to be used on all of them; then, the connection of hardware through networks

(LANs and WANS) opens the way to distributed, networked client/server-based multimedia for communication and delivery of information in all its forms to those who need it, anytime and anywhere. Such multimedia networks have already been implemented in a few schools, universities and enterprises.

Cooperation is going to increase at all levels: cooperative design and development of educational material (the term "virtual faculties" has been used) will be possible using the same networks; the result will be more material produced faster, at lower cost, and easily updated every time it is necessary.

Information highways are discussed in the USA and in some European countries; they will offer any type of information (including video, interactive TV, etc.) to everybody in a country or in a region; this will transform learning at home in a dramatic way. This includes the expected merger between the computer and television, already perceptible on a small scale through multimedia where the computer tends to become a TV, but this time on a very large basis and the other way round: the TV set will become a computer. Computer manufacturers, TV producers, software developers, cable TV carriers are already working on this. This means training at home, upon request and at a reasonable cost.

JOB TRAINING AND VOCATIONAL EDUCATION

Job training and vocational education (JTVE)s is a very appropriate means for learning and practising about health and safety. JTVE has multiple positive impacts, since it reduces work-related risks and job stress, and enhances worker's skill and employability. On-the-job training, in many instances, improves feedback in recognition and appreciation of health, hygiene and safety, and increases awareness on occupational and environmental issues. JTVE enhances workers' motivation, usefulness of safe acts, relevance of newly acquired knowledge, and increases the level of new work experience.

JTVE will surely bring appropriate knowledge to deal with potential measures, and help workers to improve working conditions and encompass the maintenance and promotion of workers' health and work performance. JTVE helps to prepare workers to adjust to a different situation, such as the maintenance and design of shift work, productivity planning and safety precautions. JTVE raises workers' and employers' knowledge for identifying problems and implementing solutions.

It is true that JTVE has an impact on reduction of injuries, improvement of safety morale, and most importantly, an intuitive understanding of health and hygiene needs. Basic education programmes and vocational training are also undeniably helpful in the full process of positive change in the working life of modern labourers. Job training and vocational education (JTVE) certainly helps workers' personal values and improves their consciousness of health and safety. JTVE can promote change in a workstation design through a change in workers' behaviour, or changes the perceptions of local workers. Control of an unhealthy environment and unsafe conditions would be easier through job training and basic education that can also lead to productivity, health and safety.

Therefore, JTVE should be pursued by first considering traditional work practice, and then, workers can gradually improve their skills to improve their work practices. Further, JTVE has to be considered as a means of action, an action that applies not only to the general workers but also to foremen, linemen and others who play a key role in defending, promoting or making decisions about the defining and transformation of work situations. It is likely that the effectiveness of JTVE will benefit more if the following matters are emphasised to:

i) promote a comprehensive skill training programme and enhance non-formal education.

ii) offer technical expertise to help setting up programmes on health and safety skills.

iii) support improved post-literacy education and integrate techno-medical consequences.

iv) promote ergonomic literacy with functional knowledge to give workers' understanding on health, hygiene and safety measures as well as ergonomics application.

v) ensure that workers are able to apply literacy skills to real opportunities in real place in real time.

vi) strengthen and develop practical courses for continuing education and skill development programmes.

vii) link learners with opportunities for employment generation, workplace improvement and safe behaviour at work

ROLE OF GOVERNMENT AND STAKEHOLDERS IN VOCATIONAL EDUCATION AND TRAINING

Today the combined forces of globalisation, technological change and liberalisation of markets are creating a more and more competitive economic environment and changing the very nature of work and work organisation. In this environment, the quality of the labour force has become a major determinant in the competitiveness and adaptability of enterprises, workers and the economy; it also poses a challenge to the vocational education and training (VET) systems to meet the rapidly and continuously changing labour market demands.

Education and training systems face a multiple challenge. Firstly, in order to equip workers who are already employed with new skills and competencies, they need to develop a system of continuous in-service training that can respond flexibly and rapidly to labour market requirements. Secondly, they need to offer young people the sound education and broad initial training that will give them a solid basis for continuing training throughout their working life. Thirdly, they must ensure access of those who are not employed the disadvantaged and at risk, to opportunities for training.

The far-reaching transformation of the global economy is compelling governments and the private sector to rethink their development strategy in general, and VET in particular. The private sector has played a major role in developing the knowledge and skills it needed, through the family, religious institutions and at the workplace. Until this century, unstructured and informal apprenticeship was the usual means of acquiring the competencies that served as a passport for entry into skilled occupations.

As a traditional and informal mode of skill acquisition for semi-skilled trades, crafts and occupations, it still predominates, particularly in the informal and rural sectors of many developing countries. This kind of informal apprenticeship, regulated only by custom and tradition, tends to be a once-in-a-lifetime experience through which existing skills are handed down rather than new skills acquired.

There are two main considerations underlying the role of the state in VET. The first is its responsibility to ensure that all citizens have access to education and training opportunities and services so that they can become useful members of society. The second revolves around the argument that, since society, as a whole is the intended beneficiary of such training, the public should bear at least part of its cost.

The main concern of the government has been providing education and training for those outside employment: initial training for young people and training for the disadvantaged.

Using schools and public institutions within the education system to impart workplace skills has taken hold only in this century, and many countries include the delivery of skills in the regular school curriculum. In most of the former centrally planned economies and in many developing countries, technical and vocational schools combine academic and technical and hands-on training.

Vocational training institutions (VTIs) have been established outside the formal education system throughout the world and may be publicly owned, or privately owned by voluntary non-profit organisations, by proprietary agencies operated for profit, or by enterprises.

Many large enterprises, recognising the importance of a well qualified labour force and dissatisfied with the quality of workers provided by the VET system, have set up their own training centres. Enterprises have continued to play a critical role both in the pre-employment training of youth through informal and organised apprenticeship and on-the-job training, while voluntary non-profit agencies have focused efforts on reaching the most disadvantaged. Yet, despite its economic importance, the role of the private sector in the provision of skills has been largely overlooked in official policy making, as has the contribution of VTIs operated by enterprises. In the case of proprietary training, in particular, the profit motive has sometimes been seen as overriding broader educational and training objectives and hence lowering the quality of delivery.

Yet, private sector institutions can respond quickly to changing requirements, adapt their curricula to their clientele, thus maintaining placement rates, while public VTIs tend to suffer from a rigid regulatory framework, a lack of accountability, entrepreneurial know-how and capital to respond to demand quickly and adequately.

The combination of on-the-job training by enterprises with vocational education and training in schools and institutions has been an important step in public/private collaboration. However, the extent of the private sector's actual involvement in the design, development and governance of VET has varied widely among countries. .

The growing recognition of the need for continuous training throughout a person's working life linked to basic education and broad-based initial training has encouraged governments to involve the private sector in the development and delivery of VET and to develop market-driven mechanisms to make it competitive and responsive to demand. A more entrepreneurial spirit has accordingly been introduced that tailors the content and delivery of training to enterprise needs, attention has been given to cost recovery and criteria have been devised to regulate the quality of the training delivered by the private sector.

Public VTIs are subjected to the same market forces as private providers and are devolved to local authorities, to sectoral or industrial bodies or to the institutes themselves so as to make training more demand-driven and to recover the cost of delivering it. Though in the face of the challenges posed by globalisation and technological change there is a clear tendency for VET to be demand-driven rather than supply-oriented and for the private sector to play a prominent and formal role in its governance and delivery, there are many intermediate stages in the transition from state-controlled, centralised and supply-driven VET to a decentralised and market-driven system dominated by the private sector. There may also be differences between sectors, industries and regions within a given country. In practice, the respective roles of government and private sector in providing VET will depend, *inter alia*, on a country's level of economic development, on the strength of its private sector and on the perception of the government's core function.

In most countries, however, public/private collaboration in the design and delivery of VET falls somewhere in between. There are several interconnected factors behind the recent moves by the state to seek the collaboration of private-sector stakeholders in VET:

i) the fiscal crisis, which has resulted in a chronic shortage of public funds to meet the increasing demand for training;
ii) the rise of the market economy and the growing recognition of the private sector's critical role in skill development;
iii) the rapid and continuous changes in technology, workplace organisation and practices and skill requirements, resulting in a demand for lifelong and continuing training and a need to reform the system of initial training;

iv) the inability of public VET systems to respond quickly to new labour market requirements.

v) New skill requirements and the need for private sector involvement.

This new society requires a different kind of learning, one that enhances trainability, thus employability. For the individual, and learning for employability means developing the capacity to find, keep and change employment, or to generate self-employment. Employable skills facilitate the vertical and horizontal mobility of workers in the labour market and their continuous adaptation to changing technology and new forms of work organisation.

For the worker, learning for employability means lifelong learning and the acquisition of competency in flexible skills that enhance mobility and job security. For the enterprise, employable skills mean that its workers are able to respond to changing workplace requirements and enhance enterprise competitivity and growth. For the state, the concept means creating a workforce with adaptable competencies that are in line with the changing demands of the labour market, as a critical factor in contributing towards the goal of full employment.

Learning, however, does not automatically lead to employability. Employability is determined more by the ability to transfer core competencies from one job to another and from one enterprise to another rather than by job-specific skills. It requires a sound educational foundation and a broad initial training upon which continuing learning can build throughout a person's working life. Certain approaches in industrialised and rapidly industrialising countries indicate a shift from the old paradigm of VET and an active search for new responses.

The nature of skill development in today's world requires closer links to the private sector. Moreover, the challenges are too complex and the available resources too scarce for any single player, be it public or private. Enterprises are market-driven and need to respond rapidly to change, they tend to possess precisely the qualities that are lacking in the state-driven VET systems, their particular strength lying in their ability to provide practical, on-the-job skills that reflect market requirements. They are, therefore, in a position to make a strategic contribution to the relevance, effectiveness and efficiency of those systems by improving the quality, capacity and productivity of the training provided. Their concern with skills development, however, is primarily driven by the short-term objective of meeting their own needs of increased productivity and better-quality goods and services.

Training provided by employers is often job-specific and focused on better skilled workers, and may not be systematic. It therefore does not necessarily enhance the flexibility and mobility of the individuals and it may not be provided in areas of long-term strategic importance to social and economic development. In addition, by its very nature, enterprise training leaves out those outside the formal employment structure, such as the unemployed, the self-employed and informal sector workers.

The role of employers' organisations can be important in voicing enterprise concern and in influencing training policy and governance, drawing attention to the need for long-term investment in continuing training and encouraging learning within enterprises. The state can contribute to enterprise effectiveness by creating a supportive environment through economic growth and employment creation. It can also promote a broader and longer-term perspective for national training policy and systems, as well as maintain a balance between considerations of efficiency and equity.

Individual workers and trainees play a vital role in managing their own learning and investing in personal development. Workers' organisations can do much to ensure access to broad-based and portable skills that enhance worker mobility. They can also give a voice to those who are outside formal employment structures—the unemployed, the self-employed, the informal sector workers—and play a critical role in creating a learning culture among workers. There are a multitude of stakeholders in VET within the government and the private sector.

The scope and effectiveness of the state's role in VET is central to, and inextricably linked with, the role of other institutions within the non-government or private sector. The power of the state lies in its legitimate use of regulatory power and in its jurisdiction over its citizens. In addition to creating an enabling environment for economic growth and employment generation, there are three core tasks in the field of VET that are specific to the government:

i) laying the foundations for, and ensuring the maintenance of, an overall national VET policy and system and regulating the system through an appropriate framework of laws and regulations;
ii) mobilising collective investment in VET and searching for incentives;
iii) protecting the public (especially vulnerable and at-risk groups) from exploitative practices and ensuring equitable access to VET opportunities.

The separation of policy, system development and financing from delivery lies at the heart of demand-led vocational education and training and increased private sector participation in VET. Private stakeholders can make an important contribution to the design and development of national VET policies and systems, such as:

a) providing relevant and uptodate information on labour market requirements and occupational information and guidance;
b) reflecting private sector concerns in the government's policy and implementation strategies and in the relevant laws and regulations;

c) ensuring the relevance of VET to labour market requirements;
d) participating in the institutional framework for policy design and training delivery;
e) determining the modes of training delivery;
f) establishing standards for certifying the quality of the training institutions, managers and teaching staff, and the level of competency imparted;
— co-financing VET;
— designing the content of VET so as to reflect labour market requirements;
— evaluating and providing feedback on the overall performance of the system.

The role of the private sector partners in designing VET policies and systems varies among countries and sectors. In many developing countries, their involvement is restricted to the presence of employers' and workers' representatives on training boards and committees. Their effectiveness in shaping VET policies and systems depends largely on the existence of a strong public policy in favour of private sector participation, the strength of the private sector institutions, their level and quality of representation, a participative culture and effective machinery to enable them to reflect their concerns and the realities of the world of work. Decentralising the design and implementation of VET by region or by industry can be an important source of dynamism, creativity and initiative that is highly responsive to local demand and changing local needs.

By mobilising all the stakeholders (enterprises, local leaders, employers, workers, training providers, educators, academics and associations), it exploits the community's private and public training resources to the full and makes the whole system more demand-driven. The role of the state in VET continues to be very important, complementing the local initiatives rather than restricting them.

The role of the state and the private sector in training is influenced by the concern of each in initial and continuing training. The primary concern of the state is to provide VET for people outside the employment structure: initial training for first-time job seekers, training for the unemployed and the disadvantaged, integration of the socially excluded into the labour markets. The main concern of enterprises is to train their own workers to achieve their particular objectives. These concerns should be reflected in the policies and state-led incentives that guide delivery. There is a growing call for the delivery function to be made subject to market forces and to be transferred increasingly from the state to private providers.

By encouraging a greater diversity of providers, competition in the open market also gives consumers a wider choice and may improve the quality of training offered. In this process, the government has to subject itself to the same incentives and competitive mechanisms as the private sector. For instance, in contracting out VET, it uses performance-based contracting, relies on market information, market assessments of quality, standards and recognition. Competitive delivery obliges public VTIs to improve their performance so that they can compete with private providers, sell their training and consultancy services and charge fees.

Markets often fail to provide sufficient incentives for individuals and enterprises to invest in training. Enterprises may be reluctant to invest in training for a number of reasons, such as wage rigidities associated with minimum wages. When they do invest, it may be in a short-term perspective and for job-specific rather than basic, broad-based skills. Fear of poaching may also discourage enterprises from investing in portable skills. Individuals—and small enterprises—may not perceive the benefits of training or may be unable to make informed decisions because of a lack of information on labour and training markets.

Private providers tend to confine themselves to training that requires low capital and little infrastructure and to focus on urban areas and on commerce and services. Their decisions may also be dictated by social demand rather than labour market needs, or by their own installed capacity.

Small enterprises have specific constraints in terms both of the delivery and utilisation of the training services offered. In-service training often concentrates on managers, the highly skilled and male workers. Individuals who may need training most may not be in a position to pay for it. In such cases, state intervention stems from its concern to promote the public interest, protect the public from unfair or disruptive competition and secure equal training opportunities for all sectors and people.

Financial incentives are the principal tool for shaping the training system and stimulating investment by private stakeholders in skill development. They also enable governments to determine the rules of the game that the public and private partners are playing, thereby influencing their behaviour so as to ensure that national, regional and sectoral goals and equity targets are achieved. Government regulatory action uses incentives to solicit greater private investment and to induce private beneficiaries to share the cost of training. Incentives give signals to training providers depending on whether training funds are disbursed on the basis of budget allocations or grants, competitive bidding or through contracts based on performance or enrolment. Incentives may be directed towards providers and consumers, enterprises, public VTIs, proprietary agencies, voluntary agencies, as well as individuals.

Funds may also be offered to consumers in the form of vouchers so that they can purchase training on the open market from any training provider. Various methods of cost recovery can be introduced to enable public providers to sell their services on the open market. The government itself may be a major purchaser of such services, thus largely determining the terms and conditions under which they are delivered. In many industrialised countries, intermediary mechanisms are established which stimulate enterprise training by acting as training brokers in a variety of ways, such as linking government and private training providers including enterprises.

Intermediate agencies provide the linkage between the government and enterprises, often on a contract basis, with payment being based on a specified output or performance linked to the placement of trainees or their attainment of a certain skill standard. Compulsory financing of training through training taxes may be used to raise the level of training beyond that which is provided by the free market and encourage a move towards the concept of lifelong learning. Under market failure, there is a case for subsidising portable/ transferable in-service training and apprenticeship training.

General tax revenues and compulsory training levies are suitable for middle and high-income countries with a sufficiently well developed private sector and administrative capacity. Such levies can be varied according to the size of the enterprise so as not to place an excessive burden on small enterprises. The levy can also be varied by sector and industry to reflect differences in training costs and conditions.

To sum up, the role of the state today is shifting from direct delivery of training to the creation of the necessary conditions to ensure the efficient operation of markets, through financial incentives and appropriate initiatives to fill any existing gaps. As the participation of the private sector in vocational education and training grows, the state increasingly assumes the role of catalyst, promoter, supporter, motivator, financer and regulator by supporting the public and private agents operating in the training market in order to satisfy unmet needs.

The promotion of an open training market frees the state from direct provision of training services and shifts its attention to governance of the VET system as a whole. The state provides the overall policy framework for training, sharing the process of decision making with its private partners while leaving maximum delivery function to the private sector. This sharing of roles and responsibilities depends on the extent to which the state is ready to delegate its perceived authority as principal actor and provider of training to the private sector, as well as the extent to which the private sector is able and willing to assume this delegated authority.

REFERENCES

Dorofeeva, N., Dubinchuk, Ivashkovsky, Tumanskaya., *Content of General education in Programmes of Agricultural Technical and Vocational Institutions*, Unesco, 1987.

Foster, P., "The vocational school fallacy in development planning", in C. A. Anderson & M. J. Bowman (Eds.,) *Education and Economic Development,* Chicago: Aldine, 1965.

Hollinshead, B., *Trends and Development of Technical and Vocational Education*, Unesco, 1990.

UNESCO and International Labour Organisation, *Technical and Vocational Education and Training*, Paris/Geneva, 1964, Para 14.

World Bank, *Vocational and Technical Education and Training: policy paper,* Washington: The World Bank, 1991.

9

Vocational Guidance and Counselling

In almost all countries, technical and vocational education is seen as a means of human resource development, leading to social and economic progress. Technical and vocational education has become a vital part of the education system and its role in the democratisation of education has been increasingly recognised.

The role of technical and vocational education is in keeping pace with new technological developments and in providing the much needed skilled manpower, especially in the developing countries, many of which indicated that budgetary constraints had limited the full development of technical and vocational education.

Vocational guidance is considered to be a very important prerequisite for developing the necessary skills and competencies in technical and vocational education. Until the recent past, educational and vocational guidance was perceived simply as the process of giving students some information about their abilities and the needs of the labour markets, so as to enable them to make appropriate decisions and occupational choices. While most of the countries responses revealed a certain uniformity in the definition of the basic concept and general objectives of vocational guidance, in many countries the vocational guidance covered a wide range of activities designed to help students while attending school to make a vocational choice, and furthermore to assist adults in seeking employment, career development and their further education and training. Throughout the countries, the nature of guidance services is more or less universal, however, the methods differ from level to level and the age groups involved.

At the lower secondary level, the vocational guidance is usually integrated into subjects such as polytechnical studies or general technical studies or technical orientation, practical arts, initiation to technology, etc. At the upper secondary level it exists as a separate subject with visits to industries, career planning, etc. At both levels this is supported by mass media and concentrates not only on students, but includes parents as well, because of the decisive role they play in the decision of their children.

The vocational guidance plays a significant role in the orientation of individuals towards acquisition of practical skills and constructive attitudes towards the world of work, enabling them to pursue specific occupations in various fields. In a number of countries there is a strongly felt need to keep pace with the newly emerging technologies, by providing vocational orientation towards these new technologies; and subsequently, the necessary training and re-training in this area.

Usually, guidance systems are organised at the national, regional and institutional level, offering mostly educational and vocational guidance services. The technical and vocational education institutions have the advantage of securing jobs for their students in many countries. Employers often seek out graduates of these institutions, because of their occupational training. On the other hand, technical and vocational education students acquire the ability to work with tools rather than with people, and therefore are not particularly adept in job search-employment interviews.

The vocational guidance services are provided at the national, local and school levels, by the responsibility of the Ministry of Education of their countries. Many countries recognise the need of individual career counselling—as a systematic process helping individuals to explore various possibilities and options and to decide, with awareness, what they want to do at different stages of the lifespan.

The vocational guidance services in many countries ensure a close cooperation between training and employment placement services, by providing information about employment opportunities in various occupational fields. Links with employers associations, trade unions and private enterprises contribute to determine the actual qualifications for different jobs.

Various countries have different approaches to provide a better access to technical and vocational subjects, a diversification of general education, adaptation to the world of work, understanding and use of new technologies, or a range of categorised approaches and priorities. In some industrialised countries, the career guidance programmes in schools incorporate a variety of information resources, including computer-assisted systems. These information resources are provided by special career centres. They usually compile available career guidance information and exploration resources, offering them to students, teachers and parents. These centres are used for research, planning, self-exploration, and group sessions, where students receive assistance in such areas as occupational planning, job entry and placement, financial aid information, and further educational opportunities.

Some countries indicated measures for coordination between technical and vocational education within the educational system and employment. Coordination between technical and vocational education and employment exists in most of them. There are usually stronger links between vocational education (part-time) and employment than full-time technical education and employment.In some countries, the vocational guidance services invite some specialists from the industrial, business, agricultural and other sectors to deliver lectures at educational establishments or to meet students and parents and provide first-hand information, which helps towards professional orientation. The transition between education and employment is facilitated in some countries.

A number of countries use a wider range of modalities to adapt their educational systems to lifelong education. In some countries, such as Denmark, the Netherlands, and the United Kingdom, there are also some private vocational guidance agencies, operating along with governmental bodies, trade unions and employers' associations. In many countries the professional orientation and guidance is provided not only to the youth, but also to adults, helping them to re-orient themselves to new occupational fields, or—for the unemployed—to find employment.

The qualifications of the vocational guidance personnel vary from country to country. In most cases, some of the teachers at the secondary level, both in the general education stream and in the technical and vocational education institutions, act as vocational guidance counsellors. In addition to their basic special and pedagogical training, they have acquired some special knowledge and skills, either with their pre-service teacher training programmes or through special pre-service and in service short term courses, encompassing educational psychology, career guidance, methodology of testing and evaluation, educational media, labour code, theory and practice of decision making, innovative methods of counselling, socio-economic development, management and administration, etc.

In some countries, guidance personnel are recruited from persons with qualification in psychology, while counselling is independent and not linked to teaching and administration. In several countries vocational guidance is carried out under the labour authorities by guidance personnel with qualifications in psychology. In many countries teachers—at all educational levels—provide attitudinal support and knowledge to enhance vocational orientation by using various materials, like films, displays, field trips, dramatisations, simulation and various games, which introduce students to concepts that will expand their occupational awareness.

TVE FOR RURAL DEVELOPMENT

Some countries promote rural development by providing special vocational courses for the rural population. Rural schools are closely linked with local communities and are directly involved in rural development projects, responding to their needs. In India, the recent government policy is to develop technologies appropriate to and adaptable with the needs of rural, informal and other unorganised sectors. A large number of technical and vocational training programmes are conducted by governmental and voluntary agencies such as Khadi and Village Industries Commission (KVIS); All India Handicrafts Board; the Departments of Rural Development and Human Resources Development. A very popular programme, launched by the Community Polytechnics, is called 'Training of Rural Youth for Self-employment' (TRYSEM), aimed particularly at training school dropouts and some adults living in rural and remote areas.

Promoting Cooperation between TVE Institutions

This issue described different modalities of cooperation between technical and vocational institutions and various industrial, business, agricultural and other enterprises. Most revealed the bilateral character of this cooperation: both the vocational education system and the enterprises benefited from their collaborative endeavours.

Educational and training institutions benefited from the physical facilities, machinery and equipment, offered for 'on-the-job' training at their premises, or assisted to equip the educational institutions with valuable equipment and machinery, along with providing the expertise of their specialists for technical advice on curriculum contents or for the design of training programmes, development of software and other instructional materials. Some specialists are also involved in part-time teaching and assist in vocational guidance, counselling, testing and evaluation.

Various enterprises benefited from the training facilities offered by vocational and technical training institutions which provided further education and upgrading of their employees through full-time short courses and part-time evening courses or weekend classes, as well as correspondence courses, instructional television programmes or other instructional materials developed by teaching personnel at technical and vocational education.

Some technical teachers and instructors are offered opportunities to participate in the research work of industrial enterprises, using their high-tech laboratories; or to work on industrial machinery in the production process so as to upgrade their knowledge and skills and keep abreast with new technological developments.

Most of the countries' Technical and Vocational Education systems have either formed effective links with industry and commerce, or are moving in this direction. Nevertheless, it is obvious that in many countries significant gaps between TVE and industry still exist. In Australia, the main thrust to promote close linkages between the vocational education and training system and industry and to encourage a collaborative approach ensuring that government funded institutions, as well as private and industry providers of technical and vocational education work together to satisfy the training needs of industry and commerce.

In each county, there is a Vocational Training Committee, the majority of whose members also come from the working life. The industries sponsor the introduction of information technology in schools, especially in the field of technical and vocational education, through some new subjects, like electronics and computer studies. Both basic training and upgrading of adults through training/refresher courses take place at the working place on full-time or part-time basis.

India offers some successful examples of cooperative training: for instance, some automobile repairs/maintenance workshops in the state of Andhra Pradesh offer their facilities for some hands-on experience to the students in automotive technician courses provided in three government/private junior colleges during the course of training.

In Karnataka State, the students of the Clock and Watch Repair course at the Mahantswamy Arts, Science and Commerce College, Hansabani, Dharwar, are sent every year from January to March for three months, intensive training to the Watch Factory in Bangalore, which offers them free lodging and lunch.

Industry and commerce contribute significantly to the development of technical and vocational education. The industry provides on-the-job training to complement institutional training. Employers release their qualified staff to participate in institutional training on part-time basis for teaching in subject areas, suffering from some shortage of qualified teachers. Employers contribute generously to technical and vocational institutions, offering awards to successful students.

Technical and vocational education curriculum is developed jointly with the active participation of industries. Industries offer facilities for apprenticeship training, and for upgrading the skills of workers or training personnel and ministry officials through seminars.

Some countries have found an effective way to train their technical manpower in new technologies through cooperation between advanced industries and training establishments, which involves:

i) Use of industrial equipment by trainers and educators on company premises;
ii) implementation of joint, cooperative programmes of research and training management systems as new and existing technologies converge;
iii) donation of specific equipment to the training institution by industrial and commercial enterprises.

The introduction of information technology in the education process has promoted:

i) the development of self-study and distance-learning programmes with open access for new clients and for the remote students;
ii) a move towards modularisation and compact blocks of study, utilising resource-based learning;
iii) linked computerised networks, offering easy access to training programme knowledge and data, as well as the opportunity of speedy updating of information; and
iv) the emergence of increasingly effective and efficient administration and management systems of technical and vocational programmes as new and existing technologies converge.

Another area of new technologies introduced within technical and vocational education systems is the computer-assisted learning (CAL). It offers the advantages of self-paced/individual learning, immediate student feedback, increased availability of uptodate information and reduced teaching load. Some of the advantages of the use of CAL are as follows:

a) use in simulators for embedded training;
b) increased flexibility of study programmes;
c) increased tutor guidance on an industrial basis, linked to accurate monitoring and detailed diagnosis of students' achievements through appropriate software.

Recent developments in electronic networks and satellite broadcasting have positive impact on technical and vocational education, but the high cost of implementation exceeds the financial means of separate institutions or industries, and calls for large scale investments for entire countries.

In most of the industrialised countries, the training in new technologies is provided within the workplace, or at the premises of technical and vocational training institutions, which are well equipped with the necessary tools to deliver such training. In cases where technical and vocational education institutions lack sufficient equipment, machinery, hardware and software to provide such training, in order to introduce new technologies some large enterprises and corporations provide the necessary funds or equipment and facilities that are needed for cooperative industry/institutional training in the use of new technologies.

In most Central and Eastern European countries the privatisation of a large part of the economic sector has severed the traditional links between educational systems and the industry. The newly emerging small enterprises usually do not have proper workshops and can offer only a limited range of training opportunities. Some private organisations are often inclined to discontinue existing vocational training programmes. Some large foreign enterprises entered these countries during the period of privatisation. Since they usually need to employ highly skilled labour that is well trained in the most uptodate technologies, they organise their own training programmes, but sometimes they also offer opportunities for cooperation with the school system, giving it a chance to modernise.

UNESCO, in cooperation with the ILO International Training Centre (Turin) launched in 1993 an initiative to increase the competence of national and regional decision makers with regard to investment in New Training Technologies (NTT), as well as in their proper selection and use. In order to raise the cost-effectiveness of NTT, UNESCO and ILO initiated through an experts meeting in December 1993 the development of "Guidelines for Selecting and Using of NTT in Technical and Vocational Education." The outcome of this joint venture will facilitate many developing countries to enter into the era of new technologies utilisation, based on previous experience and avoiding costly errors.

Many of the responding countries indicated that facilities vary from a well organised framework of institutions and financial aid for learners to a few evening courses leading to no recognised qualification. Enrolment figures show, however, that there has been an increase in all training facilities. Recent technological developments have made increased demands for mobility and skill diversification on the workforce. In Austria, for example, as well as in Germany, the dual apprenticeship system with compulsory part-time education has a long tradition. The length of the courses is extended in case of part-time schooling and shortened for those who have successfully completed some lower stage. Full-time vocational education is organised in courses of one to four year's duration.

Part-time vocational education differs from country to country. Industrialised countries usually maintain a formal apprenticeship system and a full range of shorter courses for workers, conducted in the evenings or at weekends. Part-time vocational education in developing countries remains sporadic, and less systematised. Indonesia, for instance, does not yet have any part-time courses in the formal system. In Bangladesh, organisations like Bangladesh Small and Cottage Corporation (BSCIC) provide enterprise-based and in-service training facilities. The Power Development Board (PDB) has organised training centres for power plant skilled workers employed in the maintenance of transmission and distribution lines.

Professional Preparation of Teachers for TVE

For vocational training instructors, the requirements in most cases were lower than for the technical education teachers. In the majority of cases the requirements included technical training in the subject area concerned, together with some teacher training or teaching experience. Industrial or other work experience was also generally considered as an essential prerequisite. While many industrialised countries have established national policies for the continuing professional development of technical and vocational teachers, there are countries which do not address this issue.

In some more advanced countries the national policies for professional development of teachers focus on modular and distance/open-learning units of study, accreditation of staff development programmes, computer-based learning, mentorship and integrated learning.

The ratio of teaching and training staff to learners varies from country to country, and sometimes within the country itself, depending on the availability of training facilities, time, space, safety regulations and staff numbers.

Many countries have recognised the importance of links between educational institutions and industrial and commercial enterprises in order to provide present and future teachers with practical experience in industry and commerce, thereby assuring that they acquire appropriate knowledge and skills for their teaching. At the same time there are many technical and vocational institutions that make use of more sophisticated equipment in various industrial enterprises and involve competent staff from industries for curriculum development, direct teaching and student assessment—particularly in work practice.

In some countries professionals from the industrial and commercial sector are involved in teaching at various levels of technical and vocational education courses, or in teacher-training institutions.

Staff development is considered important for improving the quality of technical and vocational education. The staff qualification differs considerably between industrialised and developing countries. In industrialised countries qualified technical personnel with several years of employment experience are recruited and given further pedagogical training in well-established in-service training programmes.

Developing countries in general suffer from shortages of qualified personnel, despite the establishment of pre-service teacher-training institutions and costly fellowship programmes. In most of the countries which have been consulted, the qualification requirements for full-time staff are generally in conformity with the Revised Recommendation concerning Technical and Vocational Education.

In many countries teaching staff has entered the profession with appropriate academic qualifications but without the necessary practical experience. In other cases, part of the teaching staff lacks the appropriate academic level of training. In both cases there are provisions for upgrading through in-service training of teachers and instructors. In industrialised countries, the recruitment of qualified technical and vocational teachers with experience in the industry is followed by special in-service programmes oriented towards special subject updating and pedagogical training.

In developing countries, there is a general shortage of both suitably qualified staff, many teachers lack relevant industrial or commercial experience. These countries suffer also from a chronic shortage of adequately trained technical manpower, and fail to attract competent and experienced specialists for their educational establishments, due to the low financial incentives in the education sector, in comparison with the in industrial, commercial and service enterprises. In general, all countries recognise the need of qualified teaching staff, possessing adequate academic and pedagogical qualifications, coupled with practical experience.

In Bangladesh the Technical Teacher Training College trains teachers for the polytechnics and other technical and vocational education institutions. The Vocational Teachers Training Institute provides training for the teachers in the vocational stream and for workshop instructors.

In Pakistan the Ministry of Education has established a National Technical Teachers Training College (NTTTC) in Islamabad with a credit from the Asian Development Bank (ADB), providing comprehensive teacher training and upgrading programmes, producing teaching/learning resources, and assisting the government in the planning and management of technical and vocational programmes.

Rapid technological progress has required a systematic approach to continuing technical and vocational teachers' upgrading and retraining. Career systems have been established to attract in-service teachers to these courses.

International Cooperation in the Field of TVE

All developing countries recognised the importance of international cooperation in providing high quality technical and vocational education, many forms of bilateral and regional cooperation, directly, or through the services of various international agencies and organisations. Some of the information gathered shows how developing countries have learned better from each other, their mutual experience being more relevant and the assistance being less expensive than learning from developed countries. The international co-operation between some countries has resulted in innovative approaches, such as:

i) Development of modules for teaching and teacher training;
ii) Use of mobile training teams;
iii) Inter-country inter-project study visits;
iv) Production of manuals and other supportive materials on workshop design and installation of equipment;
v) Setting up of regional cooperative networks for vocational innovations;
vi) Organisation of symposia for exchange of experience under UNEVOC Project, etc.

The most commonly used modalities of this cooperation are:

a) exchange of teaching staff;
b) study tours;
c) exchange of publications and research findings;
d) exchange of experience in educational management and administration;
e) development of methodologies for policy planning and assessment of students' performance;
f) development of database and information systems; and
g) networking of institutions.

In short, of the provision of educational and vocational guidance services, most of them indicate that efficient vocational guidance has not been sufficiently introduced. However, some important advances have been achieved in the assessment of the needs of extending the guidance and counselling services beyond the school population: information and advisory services have been offered also to parents, minority groups, migrants, young women and girls; along with extensive career guidance services for unemployed and underemployed adults.

Many countries recognise the need to introduce various forms of continuing education, since full-time pre-service training cannot provide all required skills and knowledge to meet the developmental needs. Rapid technological advances in the past decade have further increased the need for relevant training and retraining programmes. The introduction of various incentive schemes, such as work release, study grants, industry or state-sponsored in-service training, coupled with modular instruction techniques and distance education, have been instrumental in consolidating these concepts of continuing and flexible education in the technical and vocational field.

In countries where generally separate streams are maintained for girls in the education system, special schools and institutions are being established, where women can pursue technical studies in certain fields, while in a few cases there are ongoing efforts continue to integrate them in mainstream technical and vocational education.

The introduction of new technologies such as video, television and computers in technical and vocational education, and the inclusion of these new technologies in the curricula are essential to enable the trainees to keep pace with scientific and technological advances, especially in the field of computer technology. It is also indicated that the introduction of new technologies into the education process is costly, and generous contributions of hardware and software by various industrial and commercial enterprises, along with the support of donor agencies and organisations have helped to a great extent.

In some countries, these two functions are entrusted to different teachers, while in others there is a tendency to combine the two functions under one teacher, which is thought to bring better results. The exchange of information is seen as an important area of international cooperation. Curricula, textbooks, audiovisual aids, modular materials, computer software, research findings and policy statements are the most favoured materials for exchange. Fellowships are also appreciated as a useful means of international cooperation. Exchange of information is considered an indispensable element in developing research in technical and vocational education, and is being carried out on a large scale.

STRATEGIES FOR VOCATIONAL GUIDANCE IN THE TWENTY-FIRST CENTURY

Vocational guidance helps people accomplish the following goals whether they are learners planning their education, training and careers, or adults planning their careers or further training, or preparing to become more employable:

i) Identify own talents, strengths and weaknesses, family expectations and national requirements to sort out the personal relevance of the educational and vocational options available;

ii) Understand the available education and training options and the requirements for admission and success, and select an appropriate field of study;

iii) Understand the work options that are available, the qualifications required, the means of gaining entry, the life of the worker and the rewards of the jobs;

iv) Translate information about self, educational opportunities and the world of work into short-range and long-range career goals;

v) Learn effective job-search procedures;

vi) Develop career adaptability to be able to take advantage of opportunities as they occur;

vii) Overcome self-defeating behaviours, gain self-confidence and learn life skills;

viii) Cope with the reactions to job loss of anger, depression, frustration and apathy, and learn to take continuing positive action to become employed again; and

ix) Identify alternative occupations when current employment is in jeopardy.

Guidance is a blend of self-development and of the learning and assimilation of career, providing educational and labour market information. The development of self-confidence is often a prerequisite for taking action for one's career. The goals of guidance may be achieved via individual counselling, self-preparation, career development courses, computer-assisted guidance and internet-based guidance systems.

The first seven years of the 1990s were years of economic expansion in significant parts of Europe, North America and Asia, yet many countries worried about how well they could compete in the face of the globalisation of trade. They examined their economic and educational policies and programmes to ensure that they would have competent, competitive and even entrepreneurial workforces. Typically, their recipes for future economic success included strengthening the career guidance services for learners and for workers in the labour force. As the international economy grew more worrisome and as economic management became a priority within an increasing range of countries, the development of competent labour forces was seen as increasingly important to the future economic well- being of countries.

In the past a number of countries have followed policies that did not particularly welcome the private sector as an important part of society, but now as some governments downsize they look more and more to the private sector to provide growth in employment and to be good 'corporate citizens'. The years of neglect of the private sector is reflected in the lack of knowledge about basic labour market information. The lack of this information and the lack of occupational structures for the gathering and classification of the information have presented problems to technical and vocational educators in deciding what programmes to offer. It also presents a problem to counsellors to provide vocational guidance when very little vocational information is available.

Several countries are formulating career development guidelines to specify the characteristics of vocational maturity that people should be able to exhibit at each level of education and employment. These guidelines are then used as specifications for guidance programmes and for the evaluation of programmes. Career and personal development courses typically address the following goals:

a) Understand the importance of values, work, friends, family, income and self-fulfilment to personal and career development;

b) Develop a sense of control over one's own life and work and explore one's own abilities, potential, needs, aspirations, self-monitoring, self-defeating behaviours, self-help skills and use of resources;

c) Strengthen one's orientation to the future and identify steps to be taken, anticipate opportunities and barriers, timetable steps to the future, seek and identify opportunities, and take action;

d) Examine a variety of occupations, learn about the education and training, licensing, certification or registration, working conditions and work-lifestyle of the occupations;

e) Learn decision making and apply it to one's own career decisions including setting specific targets;

f) Examine own self-awareness and tendency to analyse past experience, including what one has and has not accomplished and the reasons for successes and disappointments;

g) Learn the job-search skills of preparing resumes, completing application forms, seeking interviews and being interviewed; and,

h) Develop the transition skills of continuously developing one's competencies in the face of adversity and opportunity, obtain information on the transferability of one's skills to new opportunities, and of engage in continuous learning.

Career education, the infusion of career and labour market information into the regular subjects of the curriculum helps make the course material more relevant to everyday life and also instills the skills of research, thinking and questioning into education. The past two decades have witnessed the growth of computer-assisted educational and career guidance systems that use interest, aptitude and preference surveys; educational and occupational information; person-occupation matching systems; and educational and vocational planning systems. Equity has become an increasingly important focus of career guidance and promises to continue to be more and more evident in career education and guidance.

Peer helping is becoming very popular in some school systems because it has been demonstrated to be effective in creating a positive peer pressure in contrast to negative peer pressure. Peers help each other in learning, social activities and career planning.

Life-skills training to inculcate problem-solving abilities and their appropriate and responsible use in the management of one's life in such areas as personal, family, education, work and leisure is becoming a feature of many programmes for youth and adults. People who feel that they can influence their own lives, communicate better, have good relationships in the home and community, and exhibit social skills appropriate to the learning and workplaces are more employable and more likely to create opportunities for self-employment.

In an effort to make guidance available to all, and noting the increasing popularity of the internet, a few affluent countries provide a full range of career, educational and labour-market information, and also career and personal planning courses, via the world wide web. In addition to information, some systems include inventories of interests and aptitudes, occupational choice systems, instructions on job search techniques, a resume generator, and even simulated job interviews. These countries like the idea of "self-serve" career guidance. The information provided by governments is often supplemented by information offered by educational institutions, employers, professional and trade associations, and other groups.

In a few jurisdictions the internet guidance programmes are supplemented with electronic mail communication with a counsellor and, in some cases, with other users through open discussion forums. Some experimentation is now underway to provide vocational counselling via interactive video conferencing on the internet. A by-product of internet-based systems is that people in any country with access to the internet can see the educational and occupational structures and opportunities in other countries and also use the guidance instruments online.

Internet connections are far from being available to most people in most countries. However, the internet delivery of career guidance will be increasingly common in the next century. Online counselling has some distinct advantages: to reach people in rural and remote areas; to serve persons with disabilities that make it difficult for them to attend an office; and to accommodate people who are apprehensive about receiving counselling face to face.

Employment is becoming increasingly fluid, work is increasingly complex, occupational boundaries are changing or dissolving, and more jobs are temporary. For these reasons, continual learning is a more important part of work. Five main elements characterise an education system that is likely to prepare students effectively for this new environment:

a) emphasis on science and technology;
b) skill standards;
c) close connection between vocational and academic education to meet the requirements of learning-intensive work;
d) links between employers and school, and;
e) workplace learning.

In some countries there is considerable pressure on students to quit school and help with the farmwork or otherwise bring supplemental income into their parents' household. Recently some countries have become increasingly active in attempting to lessen the number of dropouts—and this is quite feasible because dropping out is seldom done without prior notice on the part of the student's behaviour. A number of mechanisms have been put in place: guidance curriculum; diagnostic surveys intended to help identify students likely to drop out so that remedial steps may be taken; remedial programmes for students falling behind in their studies; teaching of study skills; the implementation of peer helping programmes to make use of positive peer pressure and to combat negative peer pressure; combined work and study programmes; and changes in school management practices to give students the same rights of grievance and appeal that is common in the workplace.

The articulation of school-based and work-based learning follows significantly different patterns from country to country. In some jurisdictions there is an almost seamless transition from the school to apprenticeship programmes. In other jurisdictions there is a complete separation between school and work. The role of guidance varies significantly according to the system. In the former it is the task of counsellors to assist students to select the appropriate types of work-based training programme and to prepare them for entry.

In jurisdictions without this articulation, the school guidance programme has often been more geared to preparing the most academically inclined students for university than to help students who will go immediately into the labour force. Frequently in cultures that separate secondary education and apprenticeship programmes parents want their children to go to university and not to prepare for the trades even though the children have indicated a preference for a trade.

Counsellors have a particular responsibility to explain to parents the many favourable aspects of a career in the trades. Increasingly in jurisdictions that do not articulate school and work-based learning, schools integrate work experience assignments as an integral part of the curriculum and seek the cooperation of local employers, unions and professional associations.

In the end, learning is a personal, developmental transformation, so it is crucial to pay attention to whether that transformation occurs, as well as to the context that will enable such a transformation.

There are common elements in vocational guidance wherever practised, there are also important differences in terms of culture, education, employment practices and occupational structures from country to country. Consequently, guidance practitioners generally need to be trained in the country in which they will practise.

When guidance is conducted by a course in career development, it is not unusual to have the course taught by regular classroom teachers who have had special preparation to teach the course. Whether it is to teach a career development curriculum or to conduct courses infused with career education the professional development of teachers should give them a basic framework for career planning and how to connect activities in the classroom to the events unfolding in the labour market.

When guidance is provided through individual counselling, however, the counsellor is expected to have specialised training in such areas as: counselling techniques; career, educational and labour market information; assessment techniques to measure skills, abilities, aptitudes, interests, values, and personality; needs assessment techniques; computer and internet systems of guidance; organising career development programmes; teaching job search techniques; establishing linkages with community-based organisations; and, public relations techniques to promote career development activities and services.

Some training for counsellors is beginning to appear on the Internet and may be expected to become increasingly available through that means. Currently there are no internationally accepted standards for guidance counsellors but the International Association for Educational and Vocational Guidance (IAEVG) is in the process of establishing a committee to draft such a standard.

International standards are increasingly important as on-line career counselling can be provided across national boundaries and therefore be immune from regulation by most, if not all, countries. Guidance consultants in ministries usually have the same training as counsellors plus competencies in programme planning and adoption strategies; guidance curriculum development; differing cultural values and their relationship to work values; unique career planning needs of minorities, women, persons with disabilities, and older persons; and alternative approaches to career planning for learners with specific needs.

The unique training of educational and vocational counsellors typically is instruction in the functioning of the labour market; the structure of the educational and training systems; how to use labour market information in the counselling interview; employability skills; and, job-search techniques. In some countries, training in these areas is needed by those who otherwise have relevant competencies.

The guidance materials often include classification and description of occupations; brochures describing various educational options and occupations; and computer-assisted guidance systems. In countries where the private sector has been traditionally ignored by the government, counsellors in the ministries have a particular responsibility to establish collaborative contacts with firms to learn about their occupations, required training, pay structures, employment practices, working conditions, work culture, etc., in order to prepare relevant and useful guidance programmes.

In many communities there is a variety of formal and non-formal education opportunities for part-time learners. Perhaps, the majority of both formal and non-formal learning projects undertaken by adults relates to work. This, it appears, is the prime motive for adult learning. Governments that want their citizens to enrol in learning projects to increase their employability might take this notion and promote a career development culture emphasising personal achievement.

A career development culture would be characterised by elements such as widespread publicity about future job opportunities and the knowledge and skills that they will require; promotion of learning opportunities; and promotion of career guidance services.

In short, technical and vocational education and training are very important means to developing a skilled labour force. Guidance helps individuals develop their full potential, identify the most appropriate training, and succeed in their education and placement in the labour market and also promote the infusion of career development concepts into academic subjects to help learners understand how the course work fits together and forms a body of knowledge and skills related to performance in work and other aspects of life.

REFERENCES

Australian Education Council, "Career Education in Australian Schools: National Goals, Student, School and System Outcomes and Evaluative Arrangements", *Curriculum Corporation*, Melbourne, Australia, 1992.

Ahm. Gillani, S. Z., "The Development of Technical and Vocational Education in Pakistan", *UNEVOC*, 1995.

Bysshe, S., "Role of Guidance in Tackling Long-Term Unemployment", *Newsletter of the International Association for Educational and Vocational Guidance*, No 33, 1998.

Bhaerman, R., H. Hoxter, "The Organisation of Educational and Vocational Guidance Services", *Unesco*, 1985.

Charter, G. A., D. Persaud, A. Poonwassie, S. Williams, D. Zinger, *Career Counselling for Aboriginal Youth: The Journey Inward; The Journey Outward*, Toronto, Guidance Centre, 1994.

Conger, D. S., "Guidance for Students with Disabilities", *Guidance & Counselling,* Vol. 12, No. 3, pp13 -19, 1977.

Killeen, J., M. White, A. G. Watts, "The Economic Value of Careers Guidance", *Learning Partnership*, 1992.

Miller, J. V., L. Vetter, "Vocational Guidance for Equal Access and Opportunity for Girls and Women in Technical and Vocational Education", *Paris, UNESCO, (UNEVOC Studies in Technical and Vocational Education 6),* 1996.

Rafique, A., "The Development of Technical and Vocational Education in Bangladesh", *UNEVOC*, 1995.

Stasz, C., "Learning How to Learn at Work", *Centerfocus*, No. 19, June, Berkeley, Calif. (National Center for Research in Vocational Education, University of California at Berkeley),1998.

Stuart, Conger, D., "Policies and Guidelines for Educational and Vocational Guidance", *UNEVOC*, 1994.

UNESCO, "A Framework for Improvement of Educational and Vocational Guidance Services for Girls and Women in Asia and the Pacific", *Bangkok, UNESCO Principal Regional Office for Asia and the Pacific*, 1987.

10

TVE: The Vision of India

The economic development of the India in general and the process of industrialisation in particular over the last four decades has brought about a sea of change in the educational scenario. The comprehensive economic reforms initiated in 1991 have intensified the pace of change in practically all sectors of the economy, with concurrent impacts on manpower needs to fill the wide variety of positions in different sectors.

The need for introduction of new technologies to keep pace with the rest of the world, to try to become industrially competitive and secure higher productivity in general are now being accepted as urgent for Indian economy as well. Although the centrally initiated reviews of reforms did not specifically refer to changes in the education and training system, the need to globalise the Indian economy and follow a market-oriented pattern of development, itself implied considerable changes in the orientation of the educator/trainers. Technical and Vocational Education and Training (TVET) has therefore become an essential means for upgrading the Indian economy and, to that extent, has drawn the attention of the industrialists, entrepreneurs and even foreign investors.

There are four levels of technical and vocational training for India, namely, graduate/postgraduate courses at the engineering/technological institutions, diploma courses in the polytechnics, vocational education courses at the 11th-12th years of schooling (general) and vocational courses at the

Industrial Training Institutes (ITIS) (Post 8th, 10th or 12th class), etc. In the New Education Policy formulated in 1986 in the Programme of Action revised in 1992; and in another Programme of Action drawn up by the Ministry of Labour in January 1995 for horizontal cooperation among Third World countries, it has been repeatedly laid down that the education and training infrastructure has to be strengthened, education technologies used, productivity improved and human capital developed to cope with the vast changes that have occurred.

However, the Ministry of Labour, at the lower end, and the Department of Education in the Ministry of HRD (Human Resource Development) at the upper end, operate the two major components of the system almost independently. The vocational training institutes, such as ITIs, have necessarily to use the products of school education since entry to ITIs requires minimum qualifications of class 8 passed for a few courses and 10 or 12 years of successful education for the rest. To this extent, the vocational training system is linked to the school education part of the education.

The past criticism about degree-level or postgraduate engineers/technologists was always that they were not the 'doers' and that their learning was not relevant to the then existing production system. In other words, it was felt that the higher level engineers/technologists were more theoretical than practical and contributed little to the production process of product quality upgrading. The education subsystem evolved to include vocational elements after the Kothari Commission (1964-1966) recommended 10+2 level. However, essentially both the subsystems are now managed by the state governments, state-level universities or state-level boards of education or training with only a limited number of higher education or training institutions run by the central government directly. That the central government ministries of labour or HRD (Department of Education) still retain significant influence/ control is partly a reflection of the financial weakness of state governments and partly their relative lack of interest in HRD issues, which yield benefits in the long term as compared to others of short-term/ immediate gains.

EDUCATIONAL PLANNING

The earlier Five Year Plans, right from the Fourth Plan (1969-74) called upon the training institutions to respond to the skilled manpower needs of industry by involving them in curricula design, provision of facilities from the industry and generally taking their advice through various committees. The Sixth Plan went farthest in this regard, demanding total linkage of the ITIs with industry. In practice, however, there had been no significant change in the situation until the onset of the current economic reforms. There has been little change in the objectives of the training subsystem between different Five-Year Plans.

The implications of market-oriented development of the economy, need for international competitiveness and general opening up, are only recently being understood. Perhaps, because industry was working in a protected environment and was able to sell whatever products or services it produced in such a market, it did not really need many innovations and R&D or even absorption of foreign technology through the process of collaboration. Now that industrial licensing has been largely abolished, industry is examining various options of competing against other producers to attract customers and, to that extent, it has started feeling the need for upgrading the quality of its products or services.

The Eighth Five Year Plan (1992-1997) visualised that in the context of new industrial policy/economic reforms, there would be greater interaction between TVET and industry, and recommended evolution of the strategy for interaction between industry and institutions, e.g., apprenticeship, consultancy, sponsored research, continuing education programmes for industry personnel, exchange of faculty with the industrial personnel, as well as involvement of industry in curricula development, etc. It recommended the model developed out of the Jawaharlal Nehru Technical University, Hyderabad, and visualised a Bureau for Industry Consultancy and Research and Development (BICARD) in universities/technological institutes of higher education, etc. At the lower end of the TVET system, it recommended re-orientation of skills to suit labour market demands and upgrading of artisan skills, promotion of self-employment and general reform of the training system in line with economic reforms.

The idea of partnership has certainly evolved in India, which has had a long tradition of socio-economic planning ever since the First Five-Year Plan was launched in April 1951. By now eight plans have already been implemented, interspersed with some annual plans during- certain periods of economic and political instability, e.g., 1966-69; 1978-80 and 1990-91. With the onset of major economic reforms in July 1991 and consensus on reduction of the role of governments in general, the informed public now expects the most powerful (so far) partner, viz., the government, to honestly share responsibilities at all levels of economic activity and not merely pay lip service to the needs, wishes and demands of other partners, namely, employers, local bodies, community, training providers, parents, students and even trade unions. In that sense, partnership now implies significant shares for these non-government economic actors in practically all aspects of the education/training system right from the drafting of the curriculum to the actual running of institutions imparting such education training.

The changing role of the state in TVET has not yet been discussed in the open, and the basic reluctance of educators to be guided by the market is yet to be overcome. Nowhere do the policy documents mention the possibilities of the TVET system being more demand driven or controlled by non-state partners such as employers, their representative bodies, employees, students, parents, local bodies or community groups, who are the other stakeholders in the delivery of TVET. The concept of partnership in the TVET system is somewhat new, unless one is willing to accept the idea of 'linkages' in policy documents as partnership.

Careful examination of both the policies and the practices clearly establishes the fact that the Indian educators or trainers have not yet been ready for the major change in the paradigm about responsibility for the system.

Various components of TVET are regulated by different wings of the government, central or state level. The upper end of the system lies in the mandate of the Department of Education in the Ministry of HRD, Government of India, where the policy-making body is called the Central Advisory Board of Education. This Board consists of the Central Minister of Education as chairman, with the state Ministers of Education, the Planning Commission and some experts as other members, and is not a statutory body.

However, since its constitution dates back to the British period and has retained its respect all along, its authority is the highest. In addition, the degree and postgraduate levels of technical education are now also controlled through the All India Council of Technical Education (AICTE) which has received a statutory status recently, also the result of the policy recommendation made in the National Policy on Education 1986. The AICTE also evaluated diploma-level education provided through polytechnics, etc.

The state governments have a concurrent responsibility with the Central Ministry of HRD (Department of Education) in the field of diploma, degree, and postgraduate education but they have full responsibility for vocational education below class 12, i.e., at the level of 10+2. There is as yet no statutory body for regulating vocational education at the national level, but the central government plays a supporting role through technical advice and financial backing, a part of which is provided through the National Council of Education Research, and Training (NCERT).

The National Policy of Education 1986 has visualised a Joint Council for Vocational Education (JCVE) at the Central Department of Education to be the Apex Body for policy planning and coordination of vocational education at the national level. The centrally sponsored scheme on Vocational Education, started in 1987, laid down its structure under the chairmanship of the Education Minister, Government of India, and this has since been established. Some standing committees were also established, but at the state level; about half the states have so far established the counterpart state councils.

The NCERT has also set up the Central Institute of Vocational Education at Bhopal as the technical wing for the Central Department of Education. In the area of vocational training at the national level, the coordinating ministry is the Central Ministry of Labour and Employment. This ministry had traditionally controlled vocational training started during the British period, but after independence two bodies were set up—one under the Apprentices Act, 1961, and the other by a resolution of the government called the National Council for Vocational Training (NCVT).

The Central Apprenticeship Council (CAC) advises the central government on all administrative and technical matters, and consists of representatives of central ministries, the planning commission, the state government, employers in the public and private sector, workers' organisations and some experts. This Council lays down standards of training in trades under the Apprentices Act and conditions of engagement of apprentices. To begin with, this Council catered to the graduates of the vocational training system only, but in 1973 this was amended to include graduates of polytechnics and engineering/technological institutions. In 1983, the graduates of the vocational stream under secondary schools 10+2 were also covered under this Council.

The AICTE is a new statutory authority for plan formulation and maintenance of standards, accreditation, funding of priority areas, monitoring and evaluation, maintaining parity or certification and awards and ensuring co-ordinated/integrated development of technical/management education. Another committee has also been set up to carry out monitoring and periodic evaluation of the technical education subsystem. The National Policy on Education 1986, after recommending the statutory form of AICTE, had recommended that commercialisation of technical and professional education should be curbed in the interest of maintaining standards, etc. The policy document also recommended an alternative system for involving private and voluntary effort in technical and professional education, in conformity with accepted norms and goals.

The Programme of Action 1992, under the policy, suggested steps for encouraging, and promoting private initiative, and support and participation in the technical education subsystem, without spelling out details of how it would be achieved. This programme recommended the formal linkages in terms of curriculum development, resource sharing, joint research projects, apprenticeship training exchange of faculty and experts on a mutual basis, consultancy and contract research, continuing education programmes, sandwich/cooperative programmes and adjunct professorships. However, no details were spelt out in the Programme of Action as to these linkages, which have been mentioned, in any case, in the Five-Year Plan documents for a long time.

In other words, the roles of different stakeholders have nowhere been indicated even in documents of the education subsystem. The vocational training subsystem or the apprenticeship programmes, as regulated by the NCVT or the CAC respectively, also do not lay down any specific role for the students, their parents, industry associations, local community or employees, etc. These stakeholders are, however, represented in the NCVT and, to that extent, it could be theoretically correct to claim that their views are heard.

However, in practice, the bureaucratic structure of NCVT does not really allow for any real partnership with the stakeholders and, in any case, the membership strength is heavily loaded against organisations/groups outside the government. The CAC may be theoretically claimed that employers of the public and private sectors, workers' organisations and the experts are represented, but this is also a bureaucratic body where membership is nominated by government nominees and the concept of partnership was hardly ever implemented.

At the state government level, the two subsystems have set up their own organisations such as directorates of technical education or directorates of vocational education or training. In a few states the two streams have been combined and called the Directorate of Technical Education and Training, as in the national capital territory of Delhi. In some states, however, the training subsystem is regulated by the directorates of industry. However, in terms of standard setting and examinations, each state now has a Board of Secondary Education which covers the vocational education subsystem. The other subsystem of diploma-level technical education is controlled at the state level through state Boards of Technical Education, which lay down standards and also conduct examinations. However, degree/ postgraduate-level education is regulated by universities in terms of standard setting and examinations.

Each state also has a State Council of Vocational Training (SCVT) which is an expert advisory board, to carry out training policy laid down by NCVT, based on the Central Ministry of Labour. Similarly, each state also has a State Apprentices Council to advise in matters relating to implementation of the Apprentices Act. Since the Apprentices Act is a Central Act, the state councils do remain answerable to the central council, much more so than what happens in the corresponding subsystem of vocational education at 10+2 level.

Further, since the training subsystem was started in the British period and was always in the concurrent list of the Indian Constitution, unlike school education which was brought into the list later on by a constitutional amendment, the SCVT is also answerable to the NCVT, much more so than in the case of the education system. In addition, the NCVT arranges trade tests and lays down the proficiency level for the award of national trade tests of the Council; it arranges for expansion of training institutions, accords recognition to training institutions for granting of the national trade test and recommends additional training facilities, where necessary.

On the other hand, the state Boards of Secondary or technical Education are statutory bodies set up at the state level through acts of local legislature and therefore are not directly answerable to the Central Department of Education, so far as vocational education at 10+2 level or diploma-level education is concerned.

The Secondary Board of Education has no partnership possibility at present with the private sector, employers, students, parents or the community. Since it is mainly a standard-setting and examination body, one can perhaps understand this, even in regard to the vocational education stream at 10+2.

However, at the non-statutory level, especially at the district level of implementation of vocational education programmes, there is greater linkage between the institutions and the district level vocational education body, on the one side, and local industry, community, parents, employers, or students, on the other. This has not been, however, formalised, and no particular responsibility has been shared by the education authorities with the rest. The reason for better linkages lies in the fact that the vocational education stream is relatively new, had been initially unpopular with people/organisations outside the education subsystem, and the education authorities often needed the support of local community/industry for getting part-time teachers, equipment and training facilities.

In fact, the shortage of trained teachers and equipment is the single largest bottleneck for vocational education at the 10+2 level and the education authorities accepted the advice and support from outside, more or less out of initial compulsion.

The relative role of these outside agents/stakeholders does vary from state to state and even varies district to district and it will not be fair to generalise any particular pattern of partnership which has come to stay in the vocational education programmes.

The polytechnic education providing diploma-level education, which is the next higher level, is different in this regard, though in some of the states the same directorate regulates both vocational education and polytechnic education. This is mainly because polytechnic education is controlled by the AICTE, on the one side, and the state government on the other. The Programme of Action 1992 under the National Policy did suggest steps to make such courses flexible, modular and credit-based, with provisions for multi-point entry, but do not spell out the idea of partnership, except in the case of what are called community polytechnics.

There are currently over 159 (Eighth Plan) community polytechnics in the country especially for the benefit of the rural youth and women, and the Programme of Action 1992 recommended further steps to improve their scope, coverage and activities. It also recommended establishing village extension centres. It promised to encourage group entrepreneurship for revival and promotion of rural crafts through community participation, as well as an Apex Coordinating Council at the national level.

Apparently, the AICTE and Department of Education are not really keen to take the community polytechnics, meant for the benefit of the rural people and women, out of the central government/AICTE, and to that extent, it is difficult to say whether local stakeholders would ever get a meaningful role in the design of curricula, running of courses, or utilisation of the facilities.

The linkages of higher--level technical institutions or degree/postgraduate education with industry, have already been covered earlier. The amount of centralisation which has taken place for so long in this area appears to be unreal in a federal country like India. The local universities do certainly affiliate the engineering college/technological institute, but the courses are designed via the AICTE though the examinations are conducted by the universities. Certifications or degrees would be naturally given through the local university, but it has no real role and, in any case, Indian public universities do not share their authority with the private sector in any way.

In practice, the state-level councils for vocational training or apprenticeship are as bureaucratic and as dominated by government nominees as at the national level. However, there are local committees at the individual ITI level consisting of the principal, local industry representatives, local employment officer, etc., which are supposed to assess the needs of the industries in the region served by the institute, and suggest measures to adapt training programmes to suit local needs. Proposals for trades to be taught at the institution are recommended by such committees to the state councils, and the authority to start new trades and issue certificates rests with the state councils, if the training programme in such trades is to last for not more than five years.

The authority of the state council is lost if the training programme is to last over five years, in which case, it is referred to the NCVT, along with results of area-wise and industry-wise surveys of employment potential for the proposed trades and information on matters such as equipment availability, collaboration from industry, etc.

Currently there is not much which can be considered real partnership among different stakeholders. At the localarea level, where 10+2 vocational schools or ITIs operate, the principals of institutions have to keep very close liaison with local industrialists, employers and others who could help in the process of making the courses useful, attractive, relevant and sometimes even captive for the benefit of some of those economic agents.

The areas of partnership under consideration could involve different levels, starting with policy formulation and moving on to administration/ financing of the system, curriculum development, certification, delivery, evaluation, etc.

In each of these areas of partnership, we can also look at the level of participation—deep, wide ranging, shallow on superficial. To begin with, the issue of policy formulation has not attracted much attention of the policy makers in regard to technical education. This is because the National Planning Commission has evolved a method of involving different stakeholders of the economy through the process of the setting up of a working group.

The education and training system of India is almost entirely in the hands of the government, though a large number of private engineering colleges, many polytechnics, some vocational schools and many ITIs also exist side by side. The Government of India, as well as state governments, run a system of grants-in-aid through which even private institutions receive grants mostly for maintenance, i.e., for staff expenditure and so on.

At the level of degree/postgraduate institutions, however, some states were quite liberal in permitting new institutions to come up and affiliate themselves with existing public universities within the state, e.g., the states of Maharashtra, Karnataka, Andhra Pradesh and Tamil Nadu. In the case of secondary schools, practically all the states ran the system of 'aided' schools for many years.

Under this system the management was all private, as also were capital facilities, including land, buildings and equipment. However, the state government accepted responsibility for tong-term funding of teaching cadres employed by the private management for ensuring standardisation of teacher qualification and standards, and developed a mechanism for reimbursing/paying up to or around 95 per cent share of cost of staff salaries each quarter. Some of these secondary schools now have a vocational stream as well and therefore the private-sector owner of the schools runs the vocational courses in 'partnership' with the state government through its various education/training officers.

Similarly, some states also evolved a pattern of private ITIs, where the state government found some money as grants but no single pattern exists in the country, unlike secondary schools where the normal pattern is of 95 per cent cost-sharing. Therefore, the privately owned ITIs certainly displayed a type of partnership where the SCVT or local directorate of training gives them basic policy guidance but administration and finance rest with the private owner.

In a highly diversified economy such as that in India, there are many institutes which do not even follow the ITI pattern of two years of teaching and training, e.g., carpet training institutes, handicrafts training centres, handloom training organisations, various health-related institutions for training of nurses, auxiliary nurses, technicians of various kinds, physiotherapists and so on, which are owned and controlled by the state departments of health in most cases, but some are privately owned by hospitals outside the government. The system of administration/financing of these specialised training institutions is bound to be different from the general run of vocational schools/training institutes of this kind. Thus, It appears that in the area of management and financing, the non-government institutions/actors have been playing a dominant role only where they receive no aid/grants from the government, but even then they can run the institutions only in partnership with the government. It is also clear that, due to recent orders from the Supreme Court of India, the privately run institutions for degree/postgraduate courses have lost some control over donations, which can have two consequences:

i) they have to raise the cost of education for others; or
ii) they may have to increase their own contribution.

In the private education institutions, the development of curricula or certification of skills acquired is done by public sector agencies which include universities for the higher end of technical education, boards of technical education for diploma level, the boards of secondary education for 10+2 vocational courses and the NCVT/SCVTs for the vocational training courses.

The AICTE, at the national level, regulates all curricula at the degree/postgraduate level. It also regulates the process of certification. In this process, the AICTE certainly takes note of the views of the private sector and educational societies and, of course, the faculty, but, as noted elsewhere, other stakeholders, including the community, the students or the parents, have hardly any role to play, even by way of consultation. This is a highly centralised system.

At the diploma level of education, general or community polytechnics, there is hardly any real participation of other stakeholders, and whatever consultation takes place is through various committees or councils, i.e., more of the 'soft' variety without any decision-making role. As regards the certification process, the education subsystem at the various levels is entirely dependent either on the public sector universities or boards of technical education which have been set up in each state but which more or less follow the instructions/advice of the AICTE.

The vocational education subsystem at the 10+2 level, the secondary boards of education control, both the curricula and certification of such courses. It has been noted elsewhere that these boards obtain advice and support from the national level partly through the technical agency of NCERT. This agency is legally a non-government research body, but almost 100 per cent financed by the Department of Education in the Ministry of HRD. While it has no real authority to impose its curricula or the process of certification on the state governments and state boards of secondary education, in practice its advice is accepted by the state agencies.

The chief reasons for this behaviour are the central government grants, since Vocalisation of Secondary Education has been a centrally sponsored scheme of the Department of Education and was approved by the Planning Commission in 1987. The NCERT advice is treated as the advice of the central government and to that extent it is considered safe for the state governments to follow it, to be able to claim the grants in time.

Further, the NCERT also lays down the methodology of testing the skills acquired by students through such vocational courses and, in the absence of well-functioning, state councils of education, research and training, the state departments find it safe and convenient to follow the NCERT advice. Very recently, however, the NCERT has set up a fully-fledged institute for vocational courses. It must be admitted that a very large amount of technical work had been performed by the NCERT, but merely toeing its line by state agencies means that they have little role to perform independent of central agencies.

The role of other stakeholders in vocational education courses, like local industry, employers and parents, is generally deeper, in the sense that their voices are heard by the principals of institutions and conveyed to the state headquarters. Such stakeholders may not be able to change the curricula for a course, but experience shows that, as in the case of Delhi, in - many states such stakeholders can help in deciding which courses to start in which school and at what time. Finally, stakeholders outside the government have been found to lack any influence on the process of certification or examinations to test skills.

The state boards of school education consider certification to be within their exclusive domain and they have hardly any participation of non-government nominees educators or education societies. In the training subsystem, the curriculum development takes place basically through the medium of NCVT, but for new courses, which are not likely to last more than five years, the SCVTs also play an important role. It has been noted that theoretically both NCVT and SCVTs have participation of non-government nominees to the extent of one-third or less.

The non-government nominees, who generally exclude students, parents or employees, can suggest inclusion of new courses, the nature of training to be offered, the equipment on which proficiency ought to be acquired and so on, but they have no decision-making role. Such decisions are naturally controlled by the Ministry of Labour at the centre or state level, officers of labour department and faculty/experts in training from the public sector ITIs. Of course, private ITIs do exist but their curriculum is determined by the same bodies at the national or state level and it is difficult to pinpoint any clear role of stakeholders other than the faculty of various ITIs, including private ITIs in this area of curriculum development or certification.

The other stakeholders, including parents, students, industrialists or employees have no contribution to make in this process, even though the principals of ITIs keep close liaison with them at the area level for various reasons. In this area there is an obvious difference between privately owned institutions and those in the public sector. As has been noted earlier, in the public sector, with institutions right from the highest postgraduate education to the lowest vocational training the government does not formally invite non-government agencies to participate in actual delivery of education.

The exceptions are the newly established vocational courses under secondary schools and ITIs, in both of which considerable liaison has existed at the area level between those, providing the training (schools or ITIs) and local industry, employers or parents. This liaison is certainly encouraged or at least tolerated by the state departments of education or training but no instructions have ever existed to give a formal decision-making type of role to such partners in the delivery of education training. The other stakeholders, including employees, students, community or small employers, have had little say even at the area level in regard to vocational education or vocational training courses. To that extent, their non-participation is the same as noticed in other levels of education, especially higher levels. The possible exception is that of community polytechnics which exist for the benefit of the rural masses or women.

As far as, the private institutions are concerned, the management body obviously controls the mode of delivery, the type of teaching staff, equipment, on-the-job training and placement in apprenticeship. The state directorates of education/training have the right to inspect institutions at diploma or lower levels and, to that extent, one can say that government departments share the responsibilities of education/training, delivery, even in private institutions. However, it will be difficult to claim that this is a formal partnership, since the legislative framework provides for the duty and responsibility of the government department to make such inspections and give corresponding advice. The public sector system, being the more extensive one, the private institutions certainly take advantage of the expertise of trainers/educators working there and they do sometimes assist the private owners in the process of recruitment, selection, training and utilisation of staff and equipment.

The Government of India has been trying to piece together new policy initiatives to involve the private sector in the education/training system after the enunciation of economic reforms in 1991. Three years ago, it was decided by the Ministry of Finance, Government of India, to give some tax benefits for investment in private institutions of higher learning. So far, the only taxation benefits a donor receives through investment in the private education system is in the nature of tax-free expenditure on R&D, which need not be performed in an education institution. There are two sections under the Income Tax Act 1961, under which donations given for research purposes can be offset against income, either to the extent of

50 per cent or 100 per cent. For the purpose of training as such, no taxation or other financial incentives have ever been given, either by the central government or state governments, so far. This is true even for in-plant training, or apprenticeship training in the workplace. The state governments have, however, operated non-statutory incentives in the form of subsidised government land for setting up education/training institutions.

One of the important problems in implementing the partnership concept is that the Indian TVET system was almost entirely driven by supply-side considerations. The partnerships attempted in India are basically of the 'soft' type, without any formal role in decision making. As the process of economic reforms proceeded, the local industry, employers and others increasingly accepted the strategic advantages of higher-quality person networkers and have therefore been discussing the methodology of developing such partnerships.

The roles of parents and students have also not been properly visualised in India at most levels of education/training. Even when the opinions about students' participation in management were strong in the 1970s, the Indian education/training institutions resisted such calls and tried to avoid any formal decision-making role going to them. The teachers and managers of the TVET system have not involved parents and students as a rule, the sole exceptions being vocational education and vocational training. At the area level, the involvement of the stakeholders has not been perceived to be in conflict with the teaching process, but this has been mostly due to the fact that the education/training system needed the assistance of the parents, students and other economic agents because of deficiencies in the system itself, e.g., shortage of teachers, equipment, training methodology, textual materials, etc.

In brief, the lack of finances, on the one side, and rising social and economic demands, on the other, will eventually ensure that other stakeholders, especially private industry, would acquire deeper and significant roles in the medium term in all the components of the TVET system.

TECHNICAL AND VOCATIONAL EDUCATION SYSTEM

In India, the Educational and Training Enterprise which operates at all conceivable levels from preschool to post-doctoral is of a monumental size. In the formal education system, the preschool years range from one to three followed by 10 years of high school and 23 years of higher secondary.

The tertiary education is of mostly three to four years for undergraduate studies followed by Masters, M.Phil and PhD degrees. There are many universities and institutions for the post-doctoral research and training. On the non-formal side the age group addressed nine to 40 under two separate programmes for school age children and adults, respectively.

The open learning system has also started functioning in the country with the establishment of the National Open School and National Open University to provide the leadership and direction. At present there are five Open Universities and four Open Schools in India. There are more than 7,40,000 formal schools. More than 3.6 million teachers are working on full-time basis. There are more than 175 universities offering undergraduate and postgraduate courses and about 6,000 colleges affiliated to these universities. The educational structure in India is generally referred to as the Ten + Two + Three (10+2+3) pattern. The first 10 years provide undifferentiated general education for all students.

The +2 stage, also known as the higher secondary or senior secondary, provides for differentiation into academic and vocational streams and marks the end of school education. In some states, the plus two stage is located in intermediate, junior or degree colleges but is not regarded as a part of the tertiary stage of education. Besides, the technician educational programme has been shown to exist after the ten-year period of general education. The location of one, year or two, year programmes of the Industrial Training Institutes have been shown at VIII+ and X+ levels followed by the apprenticeship training. The non-formal systems operating at the elementary stage, secondary stage (open school) and tertiary stage (open university) have been shown as shaded portions.

The Technical/Vocational Education and Training is multi-sectoral in nature. Each ministry/department in central as well as state governaments is responsible for manpower development in that sector. While some offer regular formal or non-formal courses, others draw from the general pool of educated and trained manpower.

The technical schools which prepare students for the lower secondary stage board examination are mainly located in the states of Maharashtra Gujarat, Andhra Pradesh, Karnataka and Kerala. There are 3,720 such schools which enrolled 314,104 students in 1987-88. In addition to the general school's curriculum for the tenth grade examination, the student is offered one vocational subject such as carpentry, blacksmithy, moulding, welding, fitting, turning, plumbing, building construction, rural technology, textile technology, wireman, etc.

These schools were started more as a feeder to polytechnics rather than for preparing young people for vocational fields. They continue today as an offshoot of the general schooling.

The higher secondary vocationalisation programme aims to develop skilled manpower through diversified courses to meet the requirements of mainly the unorganised sector, and to prepare people for the world of work in general through a large number of self-employment-oriented courses, not precluding wage employment orientation of many courses. Through diversification into production and service-oriented courses, it is desired to reduce the aimless pursuit of higher education and thereby reduce pressure from the tertiary education.

In 1989-90 there were more than 150 courses in different states which are grouped under the major areas of agriculture, business and commerce, engineering and technology health and paramedical, home science and humanities. The design consists of theory and practice relating to the vocational field, related subjects, language and general foundation studies which includes entrepreneurship.

The minimum qualification for entry into a polytechnic is grade X certificate. The courses are generally of three-year duration but a few range between two and four years. There are nearly 500 polytechnics with the annual admission capacity of 65,000. The training is mostly institutional, the curricula predominantly theory oriented and location mostly urban. They aim to meet the manpower needs of the organised sector.

The craftsman training is offered in nearly 2,000 government run or privately-managed Industrial Training Institutes. The intake capacity of these institutes amounted to about 327,000 in 1987-88. There are, in all, 64 trades of which 38 belong to the engineering group. The graduates of these courses find placement in organised public and private sector industrial and business establishments. Some of them go for self-employment also.

The ITIs offer both X+ and VIII+ level courses in nearly equal numbers. Most of the courses range in duration from one to two years. The National Council of Vocational Training is the supreme coordinating and policy-making body which awards certificates to students on completion of courses. The curriculum is highly practice-oriented and the elements of general education are kept at minimum. An ITI graduate is not eligible for university education.

At the national level, there are three councils to regulate the training programmes in their respective areas such as the Indian Nursing Council, the Indian Pharmacy Council under the Ministry of Social Welfare. In other health and paramedical areas, the health departments of the state governments conduct their own training programmes to meet their health manpower requirements. These courses, under the control of a variety of authorities, are marked by an absence of standardised course content and proficiency level, it is difficult to make an estimate of output of the health manpower training and production system. Hospital, based training, as an internal supply system, is also a prevalent mode. The curricula have little theoretical content in many situations and almost always these courses lead to a dead end in terms of opportunity for higher education.

The Indian Council of Agricultural Research is primarily concerned with graduate and postgraduate agricultural education and research. There are a few non-formal training programmes for the rural youth through the Agricultural Science Centres and Agricultural Universities. There is hardly a system for production of middle-level skilled manpower for the agricultural sector.

In some states there are some government-run agricultural schools but they often provide post-induction training to village level workers and other personnel. A manpower production system aiming at vocational development for self-employment hardly exists in India in the domain of agriculture.

The training system in the field of business and commerce is highly diverse. There are a large number of institutes and teaching shops throughout the country teaching many of the office trades and other vocations in salesmanship, marketing, etc. There is no available estimate of the size of the supply system and the quality of its products.

A brief account of some of the major Technical and Vocational Education and Training (TVET) institutions of India:

i) *Indian Institutes of Technology*: The six Indian Institutes of Technology (IITs), located at Mumbai, Delhi, Kanpur, Kharagpur, Chennai and Guwahati were set up by the Government of India as 'Institutions of National Importance'. The objective of these Institutes is to impart quality education, second to none in the world in various areas of pure and applied sciences and in engineering and technology at the under-graduate and postgraduate levels to further the advancement of knowledge through the conduct of basic and applied research in pure and applied sciences and in engineering and technology and to disseminate and transfer the knowledge so generated for the benefit of Indian industry and the other user sectors. The IITs have been acting as leaders in technology innovation, training the necessary manpower and promoting generally advanced technology in the country. They have been effective in enhancing the country's techno-economic strength and technological self-reliance. The IITs have distinguished themselves by the excellence of their undergraduates, postgraduates and research programmes in Engineering/Technology and Science. Sponsored research for different funding agencies in the public and private sectors, industrial consultancy and continuing education programmes also are areas in which the IITs have made significant contributions over the years. A special preparatory course of 10 months' duration was conducted to improve the intake of SC/ST students in the IITs. The SC/ST students were provided financial support by way of free messing, pocket allowance, loans and discretionary grants.

ii) *Indian Institute of Science, Bangalore*: The Indian Institute of Science (IISc), Bangalore, was set up in 1909 with the objective of imparting postgraduate education and carrying out research in various areas of basic science and engineering and technology. Over the years, the IISc has earned global reputation as an inspiring centre of excellence in research in all its areas of specialisation. It was given a status of Deemed University in 1958. It has succeeded in encouraging creativity, nurturing excellence and boosting innovative research and development, technology transfer and support to industrial problems. Several departments of the Institute have the dimensions of the best national laboratories in terms of productivity and linkages.

The Institute has taken up several new activities. It has introduced an integrated PhD. programme. Young students are admitted to PhD directly after their BSc. degree. The Institute offers an External Registration programme where active engineers and researchers working in industries and R&D organisations can register for a PhD degree at the Institute. There is a programme on Continuing Education involving a large number of technical personnel in and around Bangalore through its proficiency activities. The Institute has taken up a programme of technology development involving industries in the areas of Advanced Materials, Biotechnology, Information Processing and Food Processing Technologies. The Institute has recently established a Society for Innovation and Development to channellise the technological development of activities carried out at the Institute. The Institute has also taken up an activity SUTRA (Sustainable Transformation of Rural Areas) under the aegis of ASTRA (Application of Science and Technologies to Rural Areas) and in this programme, the Institute applies modern developments in technology to rural upliftment. The emphasis will be on biogasifiers, low-cost building, reappropriation of energy and water sources and such other activities.

The Institute has established a Super Computer Centre of national importance. It has microwave link with international terminals. The IISc has close links with the Department of Space and Defence Research and Development Organisation (DRDO). The Institute handles around 200 consultancy projects entrusted by industry every year. A recent assessment by UNESCO has placed the Indian Institute of Science at the eighteenth rank among universities in the world and first in the Asia-Pacific region.

iii) *Indian Institutes of Management*: Indian Institutes of Management (IIMs) located at Ahmedabad, Calcutta,

Bangalore and Lucknow are institutions of excellence, established with the objectives of imparting high quality management education and training, conducting research and providing consultancy services in the field of management to various sectors of the Indian economy. Two more IIMs, one at Indore and the other at Calicut, have also been recently established. While the IIM, Calicut, commenced its academic session from 1997-98, the IIM, Indore started academic programme from 1998-99.

The IIMs conduct Post-graduate Diploma Programmes in Management (equivalent to MBA), Fellowship Programmes in Management (equivalent to PhD), Short-term Management Development and Organisation-based Programmes as well as carry out Research and Consultancy for the industry.

These Institutes have established Research Centres to cater to the needs of non-corporate and under-managed sectors, viz., Agriculture, Rural Development, Public Systems Management, Energy, Health Education, Habitat, etc.

IIMs play a leadership role in the nation's managerial manpower development and carry out research in new emerging areas. These Institutes are recognised as premier management institutions, comparable to the best in the world for teaching, research and interaction with industries. IIMs being role models have shared knowledge and skills with other institutions to improve their quality and standards in management education. IIMs have earned an international reputation for the quality of their alumni.

iv) *Regional Engineering Colleges*: Regional Engineering Colleges (RECs) were established, one each in the major states, to meet the country's growing requirement for trained technical manpower for various developmental projects. Each of the total 17 RECs, as existing today, is a joint and cooperative enterprise of the central government and the state government of the concerned state in which the REC is situated. All the colleges conduct under-graduate courses in various branches of Engineering and Technology. Barring three RECs, all other colleges have facilities for postgraduate and doctoral programmes in Engineering, Technology and Applied Sciences. The RECs are normally affiliated to the universities in the respective region where they are located. Some of the universities have however granted academic autonomy to the respective REC, affiliated to them.

The entire non-recurring expenditure and 50 per cent of the recurring expenditure on under-graduate courses run by the RECs are borne by the Government of India, the balance 50 per cent of the recurring expenditure is met by the respective state governments. However, the entire expenditure for running PG courses in the RECs is borne by the central government.

The MHRD has taken a number of initiatives for developing curriculum in tune with the changing needs of the society and those of the industry to enable RECs to achieve excellence in education, research and development. A programme of Centres of Excellence in RECs was initiated during 1993-94 to elevate the standards of teaching, research and other activities of RECs. Through this programme, the RECs' capabilities in computer, library resources and R&D equipment have been enhanced. Such capability enhancements through improvement of infrastructural facilities would definitely pave the way for raising the academic standards of RECs as has been observed by the Monitoring Committee for RECs.

v) *All India Council for Technical Education*: The All India Council for Technical Education (AICTE) was set up in 1945 as an advisory body in the ministry. It was given a statutory status through an Act of Parliament in 1987. The main functions of the statutory AICTE include proper planning and coordinated development of technical education (including Architecture, Town Planning, Management and Pharmacy Education) in the country, qualitative improvement at all levels in relation to planned quantitative growth and regulations of the system, and maintenance of norms and standards. The Council has laid down norms and standards for diplomas, degrees and postgraduate courses in various fields. The AICTE has also issued regulations for granting approval to technical institutions, courses and programmes in the field of technical education. Under these regulations, approvals are given to private unaided technical institutions also.

A number of statutory All India Boards have been set up by the AICTE for coordination and maintenance of standards in technical education. The AICTE has also set up a National Board of Accreditation to conduct evaluation of technical institutions and its programme.

The Regional Committees at Kanpur, Chennai, Bangalore, Mumbai and Calcutta have been activated as a support system to the AICTE. Two new Regional Committees at Bhopal and Chandigarh have also been established. In order to ensure planned growth of technical education, the Council has a scheme to generate database to monitor supply and demand of engineering and technical manpower to ensure planned development of technical education.

vi) *North-Eastern Regional Institute of Science and Technology:* The North-Eastern Regional Institute of Science and Technology (NERIST), Itanagar (Arunachal Pradesh), was established in 1986 to generate skilled manpower in the field of Engineering and Technology as well as Applied Science streams for the development of the North-Eastern Region. With effect from 1994-95, the

Institute is being funded by the Department of Education. It was earlier funded through North-Eastern Council (NEC).

The NERIST was conceived as a unique institute offering a sequence of modular programmes, each of two-year duration leading to six certificates, seven diplomas and seven degrees in technology and applied sciences. The modules provide linkages with occupational levels, i.e., technicians, supervisors and engineers. The base and diploma modules provide entry to next higher module, subject to required performance of the students in lower module(s) and with the provision to undergo certain bridge courses. Thus a certain percentage of students get siphoned out either voluntarily or compulsorily at the end of each module. The thrust of this modular and innovative academic programme is to encourage a policy for vocationalisation and to allow only motivated students to go for higher studies while permitting others to go for jobs or to develop their entrepreneurial skills.

The Institute also offers two PG courses—Information Technology, and Environmental Science and Technology. Provisional affiliation to the NERIST has been accorded by North Eastern Hill University.

vii) *Sant Longowal Institute of Engineering and Technology*: The Sant Longowal Institute of Engineering and Technology (SLIET), Village Longowal, District Sangrur, Punjab is an autonomous Institute registered under the Societies Registration Act, established and fully funded by the Government of India with 500 acres of land provided by the State Government of Punjab. The courses are modular and terminal in nature of two-year duration each and are having bridge courses at appropriate levels. The Institute is offering 12 certificate courses, 10 diploma courses and eight degree courses.

The academic pattern of the Institute is designed unconventionally on the pattern of the NERIST with vertical mobility and lateral entry introduced at different levels of courses in Engineering and Technology, namely, certificate, diploma and degree in an integrated manner. The educational programmes are non- conventional, cost-effective, flexible, modular and credit-based having built-in entrepreneurship with stress on self-employment and continuity of education at various levels with provision for multipoint entry.

viii) *National Institute for Training in Industrial Engineering*: The National Institute for Training in Industrial Engineering (NITIE), Mumbai, is a national institute with the assistance of the UNDP. It is an autonomous organisation under the MHRD. It conducts long-term and short-term courses in Industrial Engineering and allied fields, industry-oriented programmes to suit the specific needs of an industry/ organisation, evolves syllabi, teaching materials, norms and standards and provides help to other institutions engaged in teaching Industrial Engineering and allied subjects. The Institute also carries out applied research, develops course material, adopts industrial engineering techniques to Indian requirements, collaborates with other institutions /organisations and professional bodies to promote industrial engineering and productivity techniques.

ix) *National Institute of Foundry and Forge Technology*: The National Institute of Foundry and Forge Technology (NIFFT), Ranchi, was established by the Government of India in collaboration with the UNDP in 1966 with the objectives to organise teaching in training programmes, conduct research and development activities in the frontier areas pertaining to foundry, forge and related technologies and provide technological consultancy guidance and documentation services to such industries. It offers (i) MTech courses in Foundry and Forge Technology and in Manufacturing Engineering, (ii) Four-year Integrated BTech Degree courses in

Manufacturing Engineering and Metallurgy and Materials Engineering, (iii) Postgraduate Diploma course in Manufacturing Engineering, (iv) Advanced Diploma course in Foundry and Forge Technology, and organises short-term refresher courses.

x) *School of Planning and Architecture*: The School of Town and Country Planning, New Delhi, was established by the Government of India in 1955 to provide facilities in education and training in the field of rural, urban and regional planning. This School was renamed as School of Planning and Architecture (SPA) after the Department of Architecture was included in 1959 to provide facilities for education in the discipline of Architecture also. In 1979, the SPA was conferred with the status of a Deemed University. The SPA has been imparting under-graduate and Postgraduate programmes in architecture and planning disciplines. The School also organises short-term courses, seminars, workshops, special programmes, and exhibitions. These are attended by senior/ middle level officers sponsored by state/central government departments, town planning organisations, development authorities, housing boards, public and private undertakings as well as institutions.

An Overseas Research and Development Centre has been established by the School to extend education and research facilities to other developing centres in Africa, SAARC and South Asia, and to support and participate in the external cultural programmes between India and other friendly countries in which the school is cited as an agency to participate in the specialised items of the cultural exchange programmes.

xi) *Technical Teachers Training Institutes*: The Technical Teachers' Training Institutes (TTTIs) at Bhopal, Calcutta, Chandigarh and Chennai were established during the mid- sixties. The objective of the Institutes is to impart training in polytechnic education. The duration of the training programme is 12 to 18 months and is offered to degree and diploma holding teachers of polytechnics in addition to providing short-term training to teachers and introducing them to curriculum development and related activities. The Institutes at Bhopal and Chennai and more recently at Chandigarh also offer PG courses in technical teaching. Besides teachers' training, these Institutes also undertake activities such as resources development, extension work, consultancy and project formulation. The TTTIs have been involved in a big way with the planning and implementation of massive state sector project on technician education with World Bank assistance. The project also provides for strengthening of TTTIs to enable them to take on the added responsibility under the project for improvement of technician professionals on a continuing basis to enable the concerned educational authorities to plan area of growth in the fields of engineering-based requirements in the country.

xii) *Educational Consultants India Limited*: Educational Consultants India Limited (Ed. CIL), was conceived and incorporated as a Public Sector Undertaking by the Government of India in 1981 under the Department of Education to offer educational consultancy and technical services in different aspects of education and human resource development not only in India but also on a global basis.

xiii) *Asian Institute of Technology Bangkok*: The Asian Institute of Technology (AIT), Bangkok, is an autonomous international graduate institute providing advanced education in Engineering, Science and allied fields. It enrols about 600 students from more than 20 countries and has international faculty members. The Institute is governed by an International Board of Trustees, whose members come from different countries along with those from India. The faculty members from India are selected by the MHRD.

xiv) *Canada-India Institutional Cooperation Project*: The Canada-India Institutional Cooperation Project (CIICP) is a technical education project mandated by a Memorandum of Understanding between the Governments of Canada and India, and funded by the Canadian International Development Agency (CIDA). The Canadian Executing Agency is the Association of Canadian Community Colleges (ACCC). This is the first major project supported by the Government of Canada in the technical education sector in India. The overall project direction is provided by the MHRD. The focus is on human resource development with special emphasis on skill development in the following areas:

a) Strategic Planning
b) Staff Development
c) Industry-Institute Interaction
d) Continuing Education
e) Management Development
f) Management Information Systems
g) Women in Development
h) Environment Development
i) Student Services
j) Equipment Repair Facility

The project is designed to foster links among the Indian and Canadian partner institutions comprising (i) the Indian Society for Technical Education (ISTE), New Delhi, (ii) Technical Teachers' Training Institute (=I), Chennai, (i ii) Directorates of Technical Education (DTEs) of Karnataka, Kerala and Tamil Nadu, (iv) 13 polytechnics in these states, (v) Association of Canadian Community Colleges (ACCC) and (vi) selected Canadian colleges and institutes.

Phase I of the Project (1991-96) was completed by March 1996. The project was extended for three years (1996-99) to achieve sustainability and transfer of responsibility to Indian partners and, accordingly, considerable inputs were provided to strengthen the DTEs in the respective states. Twelve new polytechnics from the Project States have been added in the extended period of the Project for replication of the Project outcomes.

The DTEs are developing appropriate systems and procedures to provide continued support and encouragement to the project polytechnics in all CIICP activities. In the replication polytechnics, the entire staff is showing a high level of commitment and interest in the replication process with the result that, in many instances, targets are being achieved much faster than planned or expected. Moreover, a sense of belonging, ownership and team spirit is prevailing in all Project polytechnics with respect to all Project initiatives. An abundance of good resource material and well-trained and committed resource persons on HRD-related areas are already available. The ISTE and TTTI, Chennai have been suitably strengthened. The linkages and coordination between the Indian partner institutes and organisations like MHRD, Directorates, ISTE, TTTI and the Project polytechnics are now stronger than ever before.

The Department of Education, MHRD renders all help, support, assistance, cooperation and guidance to the UT Governments/ administrations as well as to the individual degree/diploma level technical institutions in the respective Union Territories for governance and for proper planning, monitoring and implementation of academic/technical activities in each of these institutions.

At present, facilities for degree/diploma level technical education are available in 28 technical institutions functioning under the administrative control of the respective union territory administrations of (i) A&N Islands, (ii) Chandigarh, (iii) Dadra and Nagar Haveli, (iv) Daman & Diu, (v) Delhi and (vi) Pondicherry. The Department of Education, apart from providing necessary academic, administrative and technical help, support and guidance to the UT administrations, also extends its fullest cooperation to help and decide on all issues concerning academic, administrative, financial and personnel aspects associated with the individual technical institutions in the respective Union Territories.

THE ROLE OF NCERT IN TVET

The National Council of Education Research and Training (NCERT) is concerned so far only with the Higher Secondary Vocationalisation programme in formal schools. Its Department of Vocationalisation of Education, which is in the process of being converted into a Central Institute of Vocational Education, is the nodal agency for all aspects relating to curriculum development, staff development, research, evaluation and monitoring and international contacts.

The scope of the Department extends over the entire country but it has only an advisory and guiding role to perform. Having attained sufficient experience and expertise in Higher Secondary Vocationalisation programmes the department is now actively associated with the development of various types of vocational courses for the under-graduate stage of education under the auspices of the University Grants Commission.

In relation to the vocational training component under the Ministry of Labour the NCERT is represented on the National Council of Vocational Training which is the apex decision making and coordinating body for its instituttions throughout the country. Similarly, in respect of Technical Education Programme, the NCERT is represented in the All India Council of Technical Education, a statutory body to look after technical and management education in the country.

The programmes generated by NCERT which are taught in more than 5000 higher secondary schools as well as those in polytechnics and industrial training institutes, all use the contact delivery mode. However, the technical support institutions for all the above categories of institutions have accepted the significance of multimedia approach in general and distance learning mode in particular for imparting technical/vocational education and training.

With particular reference to the higher secondary courses, tile NCERT has developed some teaching-learning video films in electronics, automobile repairs and indigenous handicrafts such as tie and dye, Ikat weaving, etc. Sufficient stock of such materials are being built before schools are encouraged to use them for self-paced and individualised learning. The extent of post-secondary TVET programme is not precisely quantified in India.

The formal programmes of TVET are, by and large, directly or indirectly, state delivered. Even when private institutions are involved, they are mostly state financed. The entire enterprise, traditionally and by design, is highly subsidised, the students paying only a fraction of the public cost in the form of tuition fees.

The private cost is borne largely by the learners but on grounds of equity, certain sections get stipend and scholarships. The employers contribute hardly anything by way of cost though they are the most direct beneficiaries. The social pressures and equity considerations gravitate against the argument of de-subsidisation as a vast majority of TVET learners come from relatively weaker sections of the society.

The NCERT studies have described the present state of management system development at the centre and in various states in terms of its structure and human component. The role of a proper management system manned by personnel with proper backgrounds and experiences is well accepted but its emergence has been rather slow and often erratic. Essentially, the management system consists of four distinct categories of functions for which structures are visualised to operate at four different levels. The functions are:

a) policy and coordination,
b) administration (including supervision and financing),
c) research and development, and
d) examination and accreditation.

The four levels at which these operate are:

a) national,
b) state,
c) district, and
d) school.

In India, the Joint Council of Vocational Education (JCVE) is responsible for overall coordination of all other bodies and departments concerned with vocational education. The All India Council of Technical Education (AICTE) is a statutory body which reglates engineering and techonology, management and technician education throughout the country at the national level. The State Council of Vocational Education (SCVE) is a body with similar functions as JCVE at the state level. The District Vocational Education Committees perform the function of local coordination.

The division of Vocational Education under the Bureau of School Education and the Bureau of Technical Education in the Union Ministry of Human Resource Development provide finances and monitor the programmes of vocational education and technical education, respectively. The Regional Boards of Apprenticeship Training administer the Apprenticeship Act in respect of both technician and technician (vocational) apprentices.

Directorates of Education or their counterparts and Directorates of Technical Education of state governments are responsible for general administration and finances in their respective areas. The district vocational education offices or the district education offices provide local administration and supervision in respect of the vocationalisation programme. The principal/vice principal is the administrator concerned at the school level.

In India there is hardly any legal framework for vocational education policies as in many other countries. The Indian Constitution does not provide specific thoughts or directives on vocational education. There are no national laws to regulate the efforts in this area. The states also have not resorted to legislation on vocational education. Indian education in general is non-legislative in nature, and is a mechanism prevailing for over hundred years, the concepts and committees which were appointed from time to time. These were not statutory bodies in the sense that their recommendations could be binding on the union or state governments. They were accepted partly or wholly depending on the desire of the government in power. Scanty financial resources often proved to be the major constraint in implementation of many recommendations repeating decade after decade without being implemented or questioned. Slow and cyclic movement is what one encounters if one scans through the pages of history in this critical sector of education.

According to the national Constitution, education was a state subject till 1976. Through an amendment of the constitution it now occupies a place on the concurrent list. The union government coordinates the entire efforts in this area by laying down policies, intervening through the national planning process and using persuasion to bring about desired changes.

The National Policy on Education 1986 is a comprehensive document adopted by the parliament, and has been the instrument to guide the educational development throughout the country. It has recently been comprehensively reviewed by a national committee constituted for this purpose. The universities in the states have been established through acts passed by the state legislatures and function autonomously to regulate the tertiary stage of education. Similarly, the University Grants Commission and several central universities have been established through the Act of Parliament. Some of the Board/Councils which regulate secondary stage education have similar statutory status. There are also many national level statutory bodies which are empowered for regulating education and training in their own respective areas.

Educational policy formulation is under the overall charge of the Ministry of Human Resource Development. The Ministry is guided by the Central Advisory Board of Education (CABE) which is the national level advisory body which has, amongst others, the education ministers of all the states as members. However, in the area of overall planning for the country of which the educational planning is a part, the National Development Council (NDC) with the Prime Minister as the Chairman is the apex level body. The Planning Commission, with the Prime Minister as the Chairman, is the central executive agency for the planning process.

The formulation of policies and strategies is an extensive exercise involving consultations between various expert institutions, non-governmental agencies industries, teacher unions, students and community at large including the mass media.

In the field of general and vocational education, the National Council of Educational Research and Training (NCERT) and the National Institute of Educational planning and Administration (NIEPA) are two such apex institutions. The State Councils of Educational Research and Training (SCERT) are the principal R and D institutions in all the states.

The NCERT and many of the SCERT's have a wing or a cell of vocational education for R and D functions feeding into the process of policy formulation. These institutions function as coordinators or facilitators of wider involvement and interaction.

The programmes of TVET offered by different channels have different course structure and modalities for the development of materials. The ITI courses are largely practice- oriented with the component of general education being minimal, say, to the extent of 5 to 10 per cent. Those under the technician education are mostly theory oriented, the practice component being of the order of 30 to 40 per cent.

For the higher secondary courses, the NCERT prepares exemplar instructional materials and the states also prepare their own instructional packages. The courses developed by NCERT are based on the analysis of job requirements, and have been grouped under a common title of "Competency Based Curriculum". Both curricula and instructional materials are developed in workshops in which the employment sector personnel, curriculum experts, subject experts and classroom teachers participate. So far, these materials have been prepared on the basis of annual papers rather than modules or units suited for instruction in a semester system.

The semester system, though accepted in principle for implementation is yet to become a reality in the school sector. However, the NCERT has initiated course organisation in the form of flexible module so as to suit the semester system, and also would lead to the development of multi-skill competencies to meet the employment requirements in the rural areas.

The higher secondary programmes by design are collaborative in nature. The schools offer theoretical instruction and basics in terms of vocational practice which is followed by on-the-job training or practical training at the actual worksite. In the entire teaching-learning process the fulltime teachers are supported by a large number of part-time instructors and guest lecturers drawn from the respective employment sectors.

REFERENCES

Mishra, A. K., "The Development of Technical and Vocational Education in India", *UNEVOC*, 1995.

Finegold, D., "Institutional Incentives and Skill Creation: Preconditions for a High-Skill Equilibrium", in P. Ryan (ed.), *International Comparisons of Vocational Education and Training for Intermediate Skills*, London: Falmer Press, 1991.

Finegold, D., *The Low-Skill Equilibrium: An Institutional Analysis of Britain's Education and Training Failure*, submitted for degree, Pembroke College, Oxford, UK, 1992.

Grubb, W. N., T. Dickinson, L. Giordano, and G. Kaplan, *Betwixt and Between: Education, Skills, and Employment in Sub-Baccalaureate Labour Markets*, Berkeley, CA: National Centre for Research in Vocational Education, 1992.

Grubb, W. N., J. Kalman, M. Castellano, C. Brown, and D. Bradby, *'Readin', Writin', and 'Rithmetic One More Time: The Role of Remediation in Vocational Education and Job Training*, 1991.

__________ and L. McDonnell, "Local Systems of Vocational Education and Job Training: Diversity, Interdependence, and Effectiveness", *R-4077-NCRVE/UCB*, Santa Monica, CA: RAND, 1991

Hudis, P, D., Bradby, C. Brown, E. G. Hoachlander, K. Levesque, and S. Nachuck, *Meeting the Personnel Needs of the Health Care Industry Through Vocational Education Programs*, Berkeley, CA:National Center for Research in Vocational Education, 1992.

Lillard, L., and H. Tan, "Private Sector Training: Who Gets Itand What Are Its Effects?" *R-3331-DOL/RC*, Santa Monica, CA:RAND, 1986.

Convention on Technical and Vocational Education

(Adopted by the General Conference of UNESCO at its twenty-fifth session, Paris, 10 November 1989)

PREAMBLE

The General Conference of the United Nations Educational, Scientific and Cultural Organisation, meeting at Paris from 17 October 1989 to 16 November 1989 at its twenty-fifth session,

Recalling that it is the Organisation's constitutional duty to promote and develop education,

Recalling also the principles set forth in Articles 23 and 26 of the Universal Declaration of Human Rights which relate to the right to work and to education, the principles contained in the Convention against discrimination in Education, adopted in Paris on 14 December 1960, the International Covenant on Economic, Social and Cultural Rights and the International Covenant on Civil and Political Rights, adopted in New York on 16 December 1966 as well as the Convention on the Elimination of All Forms of Discrimination against Women, adopted by the United Nations General Assembly on 18 December 1979,

Recognising that the development of technical and vocational education should contribute to the safeguarding of peace and friendly understanding among nations,

Having noted the provisions of the Revised Recommendation concerning Technical and Vocational Education, and the Recommendation concerning Education for International Understanding, Cooperation and Peace and Education relating to Human Rights and Fundamental Freedoms, both adopted by the General Conference at its eighteenth session in 1974,

Having noted further the provisions of the Recommendation on the Development of Adult Education, adopted by the General Conference in 1976 and the Recommendation concerning the Status of Teachers, adopted by the Special Intergovernmental Conference in 1966,

Taking into account the relevant recommendations of the International Conference on Education,

Bearing in mind the provisions of the Convention (No. 142) and Recommendation (No. 150) concerning Vocational Guidance and Vocational Training in the Development of Human Resources, adopted by the International Labour Conference at its sixtieth session in 1975,

Noting further the close collaboration between Unesco and the International Labour Organisation in drawing up their respective instruments so that they pursue harmonious objectives and with a view to continuing fruitful collaboration,

Considering the need to make a special effort to promote the technical and vocational education of women and girls,

Paying special attention to the diversity of education systems and socio-economic and cultural conditions, in particular those in developing countries which need special considerations and provisions,

Considering that, in spite of this diversity, generally similar objectives are pursued and that similar problems arise in many countries, making it desirable to develop common guidelines in technical and vocational education,

Recognising that the pace of technological, social and economic development has considerably increased the need to expand and improve the technical and vocational education provided for both young people and adults,

Recognising that technical and vocational education meets the global aim of developing both individuals and societies,

Convinced of the need for the exchange of information and experiences in the development of technical and vocational education and of the desirability of strengthening international cooperation in this field,

Convinced of the utility of an international legal instrument to reinforce international collaboration in the development of technical and vocational education,

Adopts the present Convention this tenth day of November 1989:

ARTICLE 1

The Contracting States agree that:

a) for the purpose of this Convention 'technical and vocational education' refers to all forms and levels of the educational process involving, in addition to general knowledge, the study of technologies and related sciences and the acquisition of practical skills, knowhow, attitudes and understanding relating to occupations in the various sectors of economic and social life;

b) this Convention applies to all forms and levels of technical and vocational education provided in educational institutions or through cooperative programmes organised jointly by educational institutions, on the one hand, and industrial, agricultural, commercial or any other undertaking related to the world of work, on the other;

c) this Convention shall be applied in accordance with the constitutional provisions and legislation of each Contracting State.

ARTICLE 2

1. The Contracting States agree to frame policies, to define strategies and to implement, in accordance with their needs and resources, programmes and curricula for technical and vocational education designed for young people and adults, within the framework of their respective education systems, in order to enable them to acquire the knowledge and knowhow that are essential to economic and social development as well as to the personal and cultural fulfilment of the individual in society.
2. The general framework for the development of technical and vocational education shall be determined in each Contracting State by appropriate legislation or other measures indicating:

   a) the objectives to be attained in technical and vocational fields, taking into consideration economic, social and cultural development needs and the personal fulfilment of the individual;
   b) the relationship between technical and vocational education, on the one hand, and other types of education, on the other, with particular reference to horizontal and vertical articulation of programmes;
   c) the structures for administrative organisation of technical and vocational education defined by the responsible authorities;
   d) the roles of the public authorities responsible for economic, social and development planning in the various sectors of the economy and, where applicable, of professional associations, workers, employers and other interested parties.

3. The Contracting States shall guarantee that no individual who has attained the educational level for admission into technical and vocational education shall be discriminated

against on the grounds of race, colour, sex, language, religion, national or social origin, political or other opinions, economic status, birth, or on any other grounds.

The Contracting States shall work towards the right to equal access to technical and vocational education and towards equality of opportunity to study throughout the educational process.

4. The Contracting States shall pay attention to the special needs of the handicapped and other disadvantaged groups and take appropriate measures to enable these groups to benefit from technical and vocational education.

ARTICLE 3

1. The Contracting States agree to provide and develop technical and vocational education programmes that take account of:

   a) the educational, cultural and social background of the population concerned and its vocational aspirations;
   b) the technical and professional skills, knowledge and levels of qualification needed in the various sectors of the economy, and the technological and structural changes to be expected;
   c) employment opportunities and development prospects at the national, regional and local levels;
   d) protection of the environment and the common heritage of mankind;
   e) occupational health, safety and welfare.

2. Technical and vocational education should be designed to operate within a framework of open-ended and flexible structures in the context of lifelong education and provide:

   a) an introduction to technology and to the world of work for all young people within the context of general education;

b) educational and vocational guidance and information, and aptitude counselling;

c) development of an education designed for the acquisition and development of the knowledge and knowhow needed for a skilled occupation;

d) a basis for education and training that may be essential for occupational mobility, improvement of professional qualifications and updating of knowledge, skills and understanding;

e) complementary general education for those receiving initial technical and vocational training in the form of on-the-job or other training both inside and outside technical and vocational education institutions;

f) continuing education and training courses for adults with a view, in particular, to retraining as well as to supplementing and upgrading the qualifications of those whose current knowledge has become obsolete because of scientific and technological progress or changes in the employment structure or in the social and economic situation, and also for those in special circumstances.

3. Technical and vocational education programmes should meet the technical requirements of the occupational sectors concerned and also provide the general education necessary for the personal and cultural development of the individual and include, *inter alia*, social, economic and environmental concepts relevant to the occupation concerned.

4. The Contracting States agree to tender support and advice to undertakings outside educational institutions which take part in cooperative programmes of technical and vocational education.

5. At each occupational level, the competence required must be defined as clearly as possible and curricula must be continuously updated to incorporate new knowledge and technical processes.

6. In assessing the ability to carry out occupational activities and determining appropriate awards in technical and vocational education, account should be taken of both the theoretical and practical aspects of the technical field in question, and this should apply both to persons who have received training and to persons who have acquired occupational experience in employment.

ARTICLE 4

The Contracting States agree to review periodically the structure of technical and vocational education, study programmes, plans, training methods and materials, as well as forms of cooperation between the school system and the world of work, so as to ensure that they are constantly adapted to scientific and technological progress, to cultural progress and to changing employment needs in the various sectors of the economy, and that advances in educational research and innovation are taken into account with a view to application of the most effective teaching methods.

ARTICLE 5

1. The Contracting States agree that all persons teaching in the field of technical and vocational education, whether working full time or part time, should have adequate knowledge, theoretical and practical, of their professional field of competence as well as appropriate teaching skills consistent with the type and level of the courses they are required to teach.
2. Persons teaching in technical and vocational education should be given the opportunity to update their technical information, knowledge and skills through special courses, practical training periods in enterprises and any other organised form of activity involving contact with the world of work; in addition, they should be provided with

information on and training in educational innovations that may have applications in their particular discipline and be given the opportunity to participate in relevant research and development.

3. Equal employment opportunities should be offered, without discrimination, to teachers and other specialised staff in technical and vocational education and their employment conditions should be such that it is possible to attract, recruit and retain staff qualified in their areas of competence.

ARTICLE 6

To facilitate international cooperation, the Contracting States agree:

a) to encourage the collection and dissemination of information concerning innovations, ideas and experience in technical and vocational education and to participate actively in international exchanges dealing with study and teacher-training programmes, methods, equipment standards and textbooks in the field of technical and vocational education;

b) to encourage the use in technical and vocational education of international technical standards applied in industry, commerce and other sectors of the economy;

c) to promote approaches to achieving the recognition of equivalencies of qualifications acquired through technical and vocational education;

d) to encourage international exchanges of teachers, administrators and other specialists in technical and vocational education;

e) to give students from other countries, particularly from developing countries, the opportunity to receive technical and vocational education in their institutions, with a view, in particular, to facilitating the study, acquisition, adaptation, transfer and application of technology;

f) to promote cooperation in technical and vocational education between all countries, but in particular between industrialised and developing countries, in order to encourage the development of the technologies of the countries;

g) to mobilise resources for strengthening international co-operation in the field of technical and vocational education.

ARTICLE 7

The Contracting States shall specify, in periodic reports submitted to the General Conference of the United Nations Educational, Scientific and Cultural Organisation at the dates and in the form determined by it, the legislative provisions, regulations and other measures adopted by them to give effect to this Convention.

ARTICLE 8

The following provisions shall apply to those States Parties to this Convention which have a non-unitary constitutional system:

a) with regard to the provisions of this Convention, the implementation of which comes under the legal jurisdiction of the federal or central legislative power, the obligations of the federal or central government shall be the same as for those States Parties with a centralised system;

b) with regard to the provisions of this Convention, the implementation of which comes under the legal jurisdiction of federated States and constituent countries, provinces, autonomous communities or cantons that are not obliged by the general or basic constitutional system of the federation to take legislative measures, the central government shall inform the competent authorities of such States, countries, provinces, autonomous communities or cantons of the said provisions, with its recommendation for their adoption.

ARTICLE 9

Member States of Unesco may becomes Parties to this Convention, as well as non-Member States of Unesco which have been invited by Unesco's Executive Board to become Parties, by depositing with the Director-General of Unesco an instrument of ratification, acceptance, accession, or approval.

ARTICLE 10

This Convention shall enter into force three months after the third instrument referred to in Article 9 has been deposited, but solely with respect to the States that have deposited their respective instruments by that date. It shall enter into force for each other State three months after that State has deposited its instrument.

ARTICLE 11

1. Each Contracting State shall have the right to denounce this Convention by formal notification in writing to the Director-General of the United Nations Educational, Scientific and Cultural Organisation.
2. The denunciation shall take effect 12 months after the notification has been received.

ARTICLE 12

The Director-General of the United Nations Educational, Scientific and Cultural Organisation shall inform the Member

States of the Organisation, the non-Member States covered by Article 9 and also the United Nations of the deposit of all the instruments referred to in Article 9 and the denunciations provided for in Article 11.

ARTICLE 13

1. This Convention may be revised by the General Conference of the United Nations Educational, Scientific and Cultural Organisation. Such revision shall, however, be binding only on States Parties to the revised Convention.
2. Should the General Conference adopt a new Convention entailing a total or partial revision of this Convention, and unless the new Convention otherwise provides, this present Convention shall cease to be open to new States Parties from the date of entry into force of the new revised Convention.

ARTICLE 14

This Convention has been drawn up in Arabic, Chinese, English, French, Russian and Spanish, the six texts being equally authoritative.

ARTICLE 15

In conformity with Article 102 of the Charter of the United Nations, this Convention shall be registered with the Secretariat of the United Nations at the request of the Director-General of the United Nations Educational, Scientific and Cultural Organization.

Done in Paris, this sixteenth day of November 1989, in two authentic copies bearing the signature of the President of the twenty-fifth session of the General Conference and of the Director-General of the United Nations Educational, Scientific and Cultural Organisation, which shall be deposited in the archives of the United Nations Educational, Scientific and Cultural Organisation, and certified true copies of which shall be delivered to all the States referred to in Article 9 as well as to the United Nations.

Bibliography

Ahm. Gillani, S. Z., "The Development of Technical and Vocational Education in Pakistan", *UNEVOC*, 1995.

American Vocational Association, *The American Vocational Association's Recommendations for Investment in and Improvement of Vocational-Technical Education*, 1997.

Ananda, S.M., and S. Rabinowitz, *Developing a Comprehensive Occupational Certification System*, 1995.

Atkins, M. J., J. Beattie, and W. B. Dockrell, *Assessment issues in Higher education*, Sheffield, UK: Employment Department, 1993.

Australian Education Council, "Career Education in Australian Schools: National Goals, Student, School and System Outcomes and Evaluative Arrangements", *Curriculum Corporation*, Melbourne, Australia, 1992.

Bhaerman, R., H. Hoxter, "The Organisation of Educational and Vocational Guidance Services", *Unesco*, 1985.

Blanksby, V., P. Bruhn, "Technical and Vocational Education in Australia", *UNEVOC*, 1995

Border B., and C. Losh, *Occupational Skill Standards: State Development and Use Systems*, 1996.

Boud, D., *Implementing student self-assessment*, (HERDSA Green no.5), 2nd edition, Sydney, Australia: Higher Education Research and Development Society of Australia, 1992

Bysshe, S., "Role of Guidance in Tackling Long-Term Unemployment", *Newsletter of the International Association for Educational and Vocational Guidance*, No 33, 1998.

Caillods, F., "Converging trends amidst diversity vocational training systems", *International Labour Review,* Vol. 133, no. 2, Geneva, ILO, 1994.

Carnoy, M., "Efficiency and equity in vocational education and training policies", *International Labour Review, Vol. 133,* no.2, Geneva, ILO, 1994.

Charter, G. A., D. Persaud, A. Poonwassie, S. Williams, D. Zinger, *Career Counselling for Aboriginal Youth: The Journey Inward; The Journey Outward,* Toronto, Guidance Centre, 1994.

Cinterfor, ILO, "Vocational training on the threshold of the 1990s", *PHREE Background Paper Series, Document No. PHREE/91/35,* Washington, D.C.: World Bank, 1991.

Conger, D. S., "Guidance for Students with Disabilities", *Guidance & Counselling,* Vol. 12, No. 3, pp13 -19, 1977.

De Moura, Castro, C., "Training policies for the end of the century", *New trends in technical and vocational education,* Paris: UNESCO/IIEP, 1995.

Delailomaloma, N. H., "Technical and Vocational Education and Training in Fiji", *UNEVOC,* 1995.

Dempsey, R., "Resource Document, Occupational Information for the Skill Standards Projects", 1994.

Dorofeeva, N., Dubinchuk, Ivashkovsky, Tumanskaya., *Content of General education in Programmes of Agricultural Technical and Vocational Institutions,* Unesco, 1987.

Dougherty, C., "The cost-effectiveness of national training systems in developing countries", *PPR Working Paper Series,* WPS 171, Washington, D.C.: World Bank, 1989.

Dougherty, C., J. P. Tan, "Financing training, issues and options", *PRE Working paper series, WPS716,* Washington D.C.: World Bank, 1991.

Drake, K., "Interventions in market financing of training in the European Community", in Ryan, P. (ed.), *International comparisons of vocational education and training for intermediate skills,* The Falmer Press, 1991.

Eckstein, M. A., and H. J. Noah, *Secondary School Examinations: International Perspectives on Policies and Practice,* Newhaven: Yale University Press, 1993.

Eisner, E W., "Reshaping assessment in education: some criteria in search of practice", *Journal of Curriculum Studies 25* (3) 219-233., 1993.

Finegold, D., "Institutional Incentives and Skill Creation: Preconditions for a High-Skill Equilibrium", in P. Ryan (ed.), *International Comparisons of Vocational Education and Training for Intermediate Skills*, London: Falmer Press, 1991.

Finegold, D., *The Low-Skill Equilibrium: An Institutional Analysis of Britain's Education and Training Failure*, submitted for degree, Pembroke College, Oxford, UK, 1992.

Foster, P., "The vocational school fallacy in development planning", in C. A. Anderson & M. J. Bowman (Eds.,) *Education and Economic Development,* Chicago: Aldine, 1965.

Friberg, N., B. Carnstam, "The Role of Technical and Vocational Education in the Swedish Education System", *UNEVOC*, 1995.

Gasskov, V., *Alternative schemes of financial training*, Geneva: ILO, 1994.

Gomes, C., "Alternatives in vocational education finance: an example of participation by employers in Brazil", *Training and discussion papers*, No. 69, Geneva: ILO, 1991.

Grubb, W. N., J. Kalman, M. Castellano, C. Brown, and D. Bradby, *'Readin', Writin', and 'Rithmetic One More Time: The Role of Remediation in Vocational Education and Job Training*, 1991.

Grubb, W. N., T. Dickinson, L. Giordano, and G. Kaplan, *Betwixt and Between: Education, Skills, and Employment in Sub-Baccalaureate Labour Markets*, Berkeley, CA: National Centre for Research in Vocational Education, 1992.

Hagar, P., A. Gonczi, and Athanasou, J., "General issues about assessment of competence", *Assessment and Evaluation in Higher Educaiton* 19 (1) 3-16, 1994.

Hallak, J., "Investing in the future: setting educational priorities in the developing world", *Paris: UNESCO / IIEP*; Oxford: Pergamon Press, 1990.

Hegelheimer, A., *Financing of vocational training*, German Foundation for International Development (DSE), 1986.

Hollinshead, B., *Trends and Development of Technical and Vocational Education*, Unesco, 1990.

Hudis, P, D., Bradby, C. Brown, E. G. Hoachlander, K. Levesque, and S. Nachuck, *Meeting the Personnel Needs of the Health Care Industry Through Vocational Education Programs*, Berkeley, CA:National Center for Research in Vocational Education, 1992.

Killeen, J., M. White, A. G. Watts, "The Economic Value of Careers Guidance", *Learning Partnership*, 1992.

King, K., *Aid and Education in the Developing World*, 1992.

Lauglo, J., "Vocational training and the banker's faith in the private sector", *Comparative Education Review,* Vol. 36, No. 2, 1992.

Lillard, L., and H. Tan, "Private Sector Training: Who Gets Itand What Are Its Effects?" *R-3331-DOL/RC*, Santa Monica, CA:RAND, 1986.

Little, J. W., *Two Worlds: Vocational and Academic Teachers in Comprehensive High Schools*, 1992.

Miller, J. V., L. Vetter, "Vocational Guidance for Equal Access and Opportunity for Girls and Women in Technical and Vocational Education", *Paris, UNESCO, (UNEVOC Studies in Technical and Vocational Education 6),* 1996.

Mishra, A. K., "The Development of Technical and Vocational Education in India", *UNEVOC*, 1995.

Munbodh, S., "The management of industrial and vocational training: the experience of the Industrial and Vocational Training Board (Mauritius)", paper submitted at the IIEP/Prg.BS/95, Paris, 8 June 1995.

Neudorf, R., "Diagnosis of the Estonian Vocational Education System: Indicators for Evaluation and Monitoring", *Unesco, Paris, IIEP*, 1994.

Oakes, J., M. Selvin, L, Karoly, G, Guiton, *Educational Matchmaking: Academic and Vocational Tracking in Comprehensive High Schools*, 1992.

Plihal, J., M.A. Johnson, C. Bentley, C. Morgaine, T. Liang, *Integration of Vocational and Academic Education: Theory and Practice*, 1992.

Pring, R., "Liberal Education and Vocational Preparation", pp 49-78 in Barrow, &. White, (eds.) *Beyond Liberal Education: Essays in Honour of Paul H. Hirst* (London: Routledge), 1993.

Pring, R., *Closing the Gap: Liberal Education and Vocational Preparation*, London: Hodder and Stoughton, 1995.

Rafique, A., "The Development of Technical and Vocational Education in Bangladesh", *UNEVOC*, 1995.

Rowtree, D., *Assessing students: how shall we know them*, (Second edition, revised), London: Kogan Page, 1989.

Simosko, S., *Accreditation of prior learning: a practical guide for professionals*, London: Kogan Page, 1991.

Smirnov, I., "The Role of Technical and Vocational Education in the Education System of the Russian Federation", *UNEVOC*, 1995.

Stasz, C., "Learning How to Learn at Work", *Centerfocus*, No. 19, June, Berkeley, Calif. (National Center for Research in Vocational Education, University of California at Berkeley),1998.

Stuart, Conger, D., "Policies and Guidelines for Educational and Vocational Guidance", *UNEVOC*, 1994.

Tieng Fok, Hee, "The Development of Technical and Vocational Education in Malaysia", *UNEVOC*, 1995.

UNESCO and International Labour Organisation, *Technical and Vocational Education and Training*, Paris/Geneva, 1964, Para 14.

UNESCO, "A Framework for Improvement of Educational and Vocational Guidance Services for Girls and Women in Asia and the Pacific", *Bangkok, UNESCO Principal Regional Office for Asia and the Pacific*, 1987.

UNESCO, "Convention on technical and vocational education", *adopted by the General Conference at its twenty-fifth session*, 10 November, Paris, 1989.

Vidimantas Bumelis, A., V. Rimkeviciene, "Changing Teaching/ Learning Conditions in the Industrial Vocational Training Institutions and Employment Situation of Graduates in Lithuania", *Unesco: IIEP*, 1994.

Whitaker, U., *Assessing learning: standards, principles and procedures*, Philadelphia: Council for Adult and Experimential Learning.

Wills J.L., E. Rice, and R. Sheets, "An Overview of Skill Standards Systems in Education and Industry", *Systems in the U.S. and Abroad*, Volume IV, 1993.

Wilson, D., "The effectiveness of national training boards", *Training discussion paper no.110, Geneva,* Training Policies Branch, ILO, 1993.

Wolf, A., *Competency-based assessment*, Milton Keynes, U.K.: Open University Press, 1994.

World Bank, "Vocational and technical education and training", *A World Bank Policy Paper*, Washington, D.C.: World Bank, 1991.

World Bank, *Vocational and Technical Education and Training: policy paper*, Washington: The World Bank, 1991.

Index